Local Government in Early America

Local Government in Early America

The Colonial Experience and Lessons from the Founders

Brian P. Janiskee

THE CLAREMONT INSTITUTE
FOR THE STUDY OF STATESMANSHIP AND POLITICAL PHILOSOPHY

ROWMAN & LITTLEFIELD PUBLISHERS, INC.
Lanham • Boulder • New York • Oxford

Published in partnership with the Claremont Institute

Published by Rowman & Littlefield Publishers, Inc.
A wholly owned subsidiary of The Rowman & Littlefield Publishing Group, Inc.
4501 Forbes Boulevard, Suite 200, Lanham, Maryland 20706
http://www.rowmanlittlefield.com

Estover Road, Plymouth PL6 7PY, United Kingdom

Copyright © 2010 by Rowman & Littlefield Publishers, Inc.

All rights reserved. No part of this book may be reproduced in any form or by any electronic or mechanical means, including information storage and retrieval systems, without written permission from the publisher, except by a reviewer who may quote passages in a review.

British Library Cataloguing in Publication Information Available

Library of Congress Cataloging-in-Publication Data
Janiskee, Brian P., 1967–
  Local government in early America : the colonial experience and lessons from the founders / Brian P. Janiskee.
    p. cm.
  Includes bibliographical references and index.
  ISBN 978-1-4422-0134-7 (cloth : alk. paper) — ISBN 978-1-4422-0135-4 (electronic)
  1. United States—Politics and government—To 1775. 2. Local government—United States—History. 3. Democracy—United States—History. 4. Self-determination, National—United States—History. 5. United States—History—Colonial period, ca. 1600–1775. I. Title.
  JK54.J36 2010
  320.80973'09033—dc22   2009051858

⊗™ The paper used in this publication meets the minimum requirements of American National Standard for Information Sciences—Permanence of Paper for Printed Library Materials, ANSI/NISO Z39.48-1992.

Printed in the United States of America

To Jennifer, Katherine, Alexandra, and Mary for their love, patience, and—thankfully—sense of humor.

Table of Contents

Foreword	ix
Preface	xi
Introduction	1
Chapter 1 The Colonies of New England	13
Chapter 2 The Middle and Southern Colonies	47
Chapter 3 The Founders on Local Government	83
Chapter 4 All Local Politics is National	125
Appendix	153
Bibliography	159
About the Author	177
About the Claremont Institute	179
Index	181

Foreword

National, state, and local governments serve different functions, but are united by a common purpose: to secure the natural rights of Americans and to provide the conditions of a free society. These purposes of government are stated best in the Declaration of Independence. Governments are instituted among men to secure life, liberty, and the pursuit of happiness.

For all their differences, one thing American conservatives and liberals have in common is a healthy attachment to local government, especially as exemplified by the small towns of New England. For conservatives, the small town and its decentralized government holds romantic appeal as the repository of patriotism and conservative sensibilities, and for a rootedness leading to the sound political health of the regime. For their part, liberals have tended to admire and romanticize the democratic character of local government, and in particular the New England tradition of town meetings.

Yet there exists some risk in the nostalgia for local government, which Brian Janiskee spells out in the present volume. Recognized well by our country's Founders, that risk consists of the fact that even the best and smallest local governments were every bit as capable of violating the rights and liberties of others as their counterparts in the governments of cities, states and nations. Democratic forms alone are no guarantee against what James Madison called the tyranny of the majority.

In our time this has proved particularly the case with respect to property rights. Professor Janiskee's book represents an important contribution in reminding us of the Founders' understanding of the proper role and function of local government. The history and writings of the Founders remind us that the jealousy of a free people for their liberties must always be awake, at all levels of government—national, state, and local.

Brian T. Kennedy
President
The Claremont Institute

PREFACE

This book is part of an overall project that began in October of 2000 with the celebration of California's Sesquicentennial. In honor of this anniversary, the Claremont Institute, under the leadership of its late President Tom Silver, hosted a conference entitled "Democracy in California: Sesquicentennial Reflections on Equality and Liberty in the Golden State." I was invited to present a paper at this conference on the subject of local government in California. In the preparation of this paper, I developed a greater appreciation for the difficult conditions in which local government exists today. Hence, the title of this paper, as presented at the conference, was "The Problem of Local Government in California." An updated version of this paper eventually appeared in *Nexus*, volume 6 (2001), the public policy journal of the Chapman University School of Law. The main "problem" was the tangle of confused jurisdictions and boundaries that local governments have in the Golden State—and elsewhere—and the scholarly perception of this mess within the political science literature.

The tangled web of local government in California has arguably aided the advancement of the administrative state or, at the very least, abetted the inert response of local governments to the centralizing encroachments of national and state governments. Yet, those sympathetic to a Progressive understanding of American politics were the harshest critics of the confusing structure of American local government while those who understood themselves as the intellectual heirs of the American Founding defended the chaos. Something was surely amiss.

Along with co-author Ken Masugi, I commenced upon a further exploration of this question in *Democracy in California,* first published by Rowman & Littlefield in 2003. Further analysis of this question revealed that, simply put, neither side of this debate—despite their orientation for or against the Founders—had engaged in a sustained analysis of the specific observations of key Founders on local government. My initial examination of the Founders' analysis on this question—with particular attention to Jefferson—was published in 2004: "The Structure of American Local Government," *Perspectives on Political Science,* volume 33. After that I explored the strong American tradition of local government through an analysis of local prosecutorial discretion in death penalty cases. This work was published in *The Journal for the Advancement of Criminal Justice* in 2008.

Local Government in Early America represents the latest step in this project. At the very least, I hope to have turned the discussion of local government in America toward a discussion of local government and the American Founding.

I am grateful for the support of the Golden State Center for State and Local Government at the Claremont Institute. In particular, I wish to acknowledge the support of the Center's Senior Counsel, Howard F. Ahmanson, Jr. Mr. Ahmanson's generosity extends far beyond the material. He is genuinely engaged with the great questions of self-government, especially as they apply to local government. Mr. Ahmanson and I have had a long-running exchange on these questions. Our discussions, whether formal or informal, have been lively and of great benefit to me as I have worked out the details of this project. I am also indebted to Ken Masugi, former Director of the Golden State Center for State and Local Government. Ken is a friend, mentor, and colleague and I am blessed to have worked with such a fine person for all of these years. Ken made the resources of the Center available to me as I worked on this book. In addition, I offer my thanks to Brian Kennedy, President of the Claremont Institute, and Bruce Sanborn, Chairman of the Institute's Board of Directors. Brian and Bruce have provided for a scholarly and intellectual environment at the Institute that is second-to-none. Not only are they able administrators and counselors, they care deeply about the mission of the Institute, which is the restoration of the principles of the American Founding to their rightful place in our national life.

Dan Palm of Azusa Pacific University and Fran Erler were a great help as this project came to completion. They spent many long hours reading the manuscript and providing helpful suggestions and improvements. Valuable assistance was also provided by Bob Gransden, Conor Friedersdorf, Ami Naramor, Josiah Hersey, Matthew Peterson, and Lindsay White of the Claremont Institute. They handled their assignments with professionalism and enthusiasm and I was fortunate to have them on my team. Without the support of my colleagues and friends at the Institute, this book would not have been possible.

I also thank California State University, San Bernardino, for funding a semester sabbatical during the 2004-2005 academic year, which allowed me to get this work off the ground. I would also like to recognize the University for its support of faculty research efforts in general. A special thanks to my colleagues in the Department of Political Science at California State, San Bernardino, for their support, including our department secretary, Marilyn Gareis, who provided the necessary administrative assistance to bring this work to completion. I would also like to recognize the efforts of my research assistant at California State, Meghan Taunton, whose efforts—particularly in the early stages—allowed the project to move forward at a timely pace.

My deepest appreciation goes to my lovely wife Jennifer and our daughters, Katherine, Alexandra, and Mary. Their love, patience, understanding, and support made all the difference as I worked to bring this project to completion.

Finally, I thank those who reviewed the manuscript for their comments and suggestions. The following—in alphabetical order—read the entire manuscript: Ed Erler, Fran Erler, Tom Karako, Brian Kennedy, Ken Masugi, Dan Palm, and Bill Voegeli. In addition, I would like to thank the anonymous reviewers for their suggestions, insights, and—in some cases—challenges to the thesis of this project. Of course, any errors that may remain in this work are the sole responsibility of the author.

✱ ✱ ✱

This book is directed at anyone interested in the vital political questions that emerge from the design and form of early American local governments. The book contains an introduction and four chapters. Chapter One contains a description of colonial government in New England. Chapter Two is devoted to the Middle and Southern Colonies. The observations of key Founders on local government are described and analyzed in Chapter Three. Finally, some reflections on the nature of local government are offered in Chapter Four.

INTRODUCTION

Traveling the United States in the early 1830s, Alexis de Tocqueville was fascinated with American local government, and the New England model in particular. In his monumental study, *Democracy in America*, published a few years later, he observed that:

> The inhabitant of New England is attached to his township not so much because he was born there as because he sees in that township a free and strong corporation that he is a part of and that is worth his trouble to seek and direct...the New England township is so constituted that it can serve as the home of lively affections, and at the same time nothing is next to it that strongly attracts the ambitious passions of the human heart.[1]

Today, many Americans look upon local town governments with romantic nostalgia. This romantic ideal has been encouraged by political scientists and historians as a model of participatory democracy. Even though such gatherings as they exist today are often highly scripted, the New England-style "town meeting" is widely considered an ideal forum for political debates. The vigor of local governments in the past is held up as a model for deference to such governments today. Practically speaking, this means that local governments should be freed from both inconvenient structural checks as well as limitations on their power based on the natural rights of those they govern. Yet today's local governments frequently abuse individual rights, most visibly in the heavy-handed regulation and seizure of private property.

The writings and experiences of the American Founders urge us to question incautiously romantic notions of government. The prudent jealousy these men had for liberty and natural rights surely applied to all levels of government—national, state, and local—but several of the Founders also wrote specifically on the dangers to liberty that they saw at the local level, including those in the idealized townships that Tocqueville would praise a few decades later.

By studying the American Founders' writings, and those of John Adams and Thomas Jefferson in particular, we find that many of those qualities that made colonial local governments so democratic also made them quite vulnerable to tyranny. In *The Federalist*, James Madison called this the "tyranny of the majority," which he found to be characteristic of small democracies. Although the Founders would perhaps have agreed with much of Tocqueville's argument that local government can encourage civic participation, they were well aware of the actual record of American towns and local government as susceptible to petty despotism. Modern examples include overzealous zoning regulations that deny property owners fair use of their land, the destruction of neighborhoods for redevelopment projects of questionable merit, and threats against religious liberty by tax-hungry local officials who covet the prime real estate upon which many churches have been built. By consulting the Founders, we can discover their assessment of local government's proper role, character, and dangers—an assessment that has been largely forgotten. In order to understand what the Founders thought of early local government, of course, one must appreciate the local political institutions themselves, and the larger political structure within each colony. The Founders were intimately familiar with the several colonial governments, and made specific observations about their history and experiences. Analyzing the writings of key Founders leads us on an ascent from day-to-day municipal functions to the role local governments play in our overall polity. Our review of colonial systems will highlight both the structures that made possible the provision of basic municipal necessities and the contribution of these structures to each colony's ability to participate in the broader political controversies of the time.

The first two chapters of the present work consider the New England, Middle, and Southern Colonies, and how local governments differed in these regions. Our examination spans the period from the founding of each colony to the start of the American Revolution in the 1770s. This approach is useful for two reasons. In the first place, the structure of local government inherited from the colonial experience remained largely intact until the first decades of the nineteenth century. One cannot understand these local systems without an appreciation of the structure of colonial institutions. Second, the Founders saw the American Revolution as an event that revealed the fundamental character of local government. We find that Adams and Jefferson appreciated the New England systems more than other local government arrangements for their ability to act as a first line of defense when crises arose. In the final chapter we examine modern examples of local government abuse of individual liberties, especially private property rights.

The Setting for Colonial America

The colonial towns of Boston, Newport, New York, Philadelphia, and Charleston stood at the western terminus of an empire, at the heart of which was the ancient walled city of London. The remote Royal authorities, when they deigned to think of the American colonists, considered them lower-class plantation dwellers. In fact, during most of the colonial period, the Crown's attention was fixed squarely on the West Indies.[2] When, in the mid-eighteenth century, the Crown began paying closer attention to America, the colonists found the attention greatly unwanted and freed themselves from the imperial center of gravity.[3]

The American colonial towns were "cities in the wilderness."[4] This wilderness played a prominent role in the way in which Americans came to view not just the city in particular, but local government generally, as Americans built their cities with the knowledge that there existed a seemingly inexhaustible wilderness into which they could expand.[5]

Unlike Europe, walled cities did not exist in America—an important distinction, for it reminds us that the center of the American town was not static.[6] The characteristics of a drifting center and an apparently boundless frontier helped to foster a vision of urban space that was truly unique—truly American.[7]

Life on the frontier offered the colonists an opportunity to make their way in the world, to become prosperous and virtuous. This life presented the possibility of great renewal and sanctification. With opportunity came danger. While the hazards of starvation lessened considerably within the first decade of settlement, disease and war remained constant threats. Smallpox, dysentery, typhoid, diphtheria, and yellow fever—among other maladies—afflicted America throughout the colonial period. To make matters worse, the colonists found themselves in a near-constant state of war with the French, Indians, or some combination thereof. Thus early American local government must be understood in the context of isolation and danger.

In spite of these conditions, local governments were generally successful in attending to their many municipal duties. The towns, parishes, and counties that formed the structure of colonial local government were responsible for arming and provisioning troops, handling claims of religious heresy, mollifying political fallout from dynastic succession struggles in the home government, designating land titles, arranging means of communication, making internal improvements, education, temperance, care for the poor and infirm, division and preservation of public lands, taxation, and managing municipal debt. John Adams' great-grandson Charles Francis Adams, Jr., in his research on early American local government, rightly noted that these responsibilities were worthy of statesmen, much less local officials.[8] It could indeed be argued that all—or most—politics was local during the colonial period.

The Origins and Structure of American Local Government

How did such a robust system of local government eventually develop in America? In the late nineteenth century, influential historians Herbert Baxter Adams and Lois Kimball Matthews proposed that America's strong system of local government results from the Germanic blood that flowed in the veins of so many of the early colonists.[9] The American town, they argued, derived from the German *tun* of the fourth and fifth centuries, transmitted to America by way of the English Saxons. This form of government was interwoven with English political life so closely that even the eleventh century Norman conquerors themselves were unable to displace it.[10] The English system of local government reached its apogee in the chartered cities of the fifteenth century, and it is this model, according to Adams and Matthews, upon which the colonists constructed the American system of local rule.[11]

By contrast, James Wilson and George Bryan—a Federalist and an Anti-Federalist, respectively—had agreed that Saxon government was a model for American institutions; but both writers cited the Saxons as a particular group that availed itself of universal rather than ethnic principles. A strong system of local government was not a Saxon principle, but a principle that the Saxons—or a variety of peoples—could have implemented. Accordingly, Saxon ethnicity was not the source of their liberty. Thus, there is little in the works of Wilson or Bryan to support the implicit Social Darwinism that lies at the heart of the Germanic origins thesis.[12]

Subsequent commentators have also cast doubt upon the Germanic theory of the development of local government in America. Frederick Jackson Turner argued that American political institutions and social mores were the product of the American encounter with the wilderness.[13] The open frontier had acted as safety valve for American society, releasing the pressure that could have potentially crushed the fledgling regime. Furthermore, with each significant westward movement, this migratory population became, in a political and cultural sense, less dependent upon European tradition for guidance. The frontier contributed to American exceptionalism.[14] Turner, however, also had his critics.

Turner's theory may have underestimated the power of ideas, focusing too closely on the frontier-as-standing-reserve. While the frontier was an important factor in American development, Turner's "frontier thesis" arguably takes too lightly the Founding's intellectual heritage. After all, the phenomenon of the frontier may have been fruitless for the development of local democracy without the Americans' embrace of social compact theory, which holds that all governments should be judged by how well they secure certain fundamental liberties of the governed. Russia has a vast frontier, yet its history is bereft of significant democratic development.[15] One can also hardly discount the influence of Calvinist Protestantism in the development of strong local institutions. The concept of the priesthood of all believers, at the very least, was consistent with a polity made up of a network of towns, each with its own independent church congregation. This rings particularly true for New England town government, where the Calvinist influence was most deeply felt.[16]

Assessing Forms and Structure

While early local governments were often quite *democratic*, they were not the bastions of religious and political liberty we usually assume today. Democracy, defined properly as rule by the majority, is by no means synonymous with free government which respects the natural rights of all, including the minority. In fact, the great participatory features of the New England town were made possible by a rather brutally enforced Puritanical homogeneity. Local government was the strongest where the dangers were greatest, the belief in the social compact most prevalent, and the Calvinist faith most ardent. It appears that the more potent the mixture of these characteristics, the more likely it was that colonial towns would be truly self-governing.

New England town government is arguably the colonial local government structure most familiar to modern observers. This form of government was made possible by the social cohesion that existed in early New England society (*ca.* 1630-1680). This cohesion was due to religious and social homogeneity among the Puritans, which was maintained by very strict measures.[17] An individual's application for town membership required approval by a town meeting vote.

Applications were judged in light of the petitioner's adherence to Puritan orthodoxy and the ability of the candidate to provide for himself and his family. The applicant's moral character had to be vouched for in a letter from an official in his hometown. The unorthodox received approval only rarely, and those who were poor or without good character references were turned down.[18]

For all of the praise the New England town receives today among political scientists, there is scant discussion of this often brutal legacy.[19] Ostracism, public whippings, and even executions for heresy were employed by the towns to maintain homogeneity. This is not to say that modern observers should scoff at the democratic nature of the New England towns. We must, however, be mindful of the questionable methods by which these towns were able to successfully create New England democracy. Democracy by majority rule can sometimes be illiberal and harsh.

Madison's analysis in *The Federalist* No. 10 is best known as a hearty refutation of the Anti-Federalists' "small republic" argument during the debate over constitutional ratification. It can be applied just as pointedly to the New England town:

> [From this view of the subject it may be concluded that] a pure democracy, by which I mean a society consisting of a small number of citizens, who assemble and administer the government in person, can admit of no cure for the mischiefs of faction. A common passion or interest will, in almost every case, be felt by a majority of the whole; a communication and concert results from the form of government itself; and there is nothing to check the inducements to sacrifice the weaker party or an obnoxious individual. Hence it is that such democracies have ever been found incompatible with personal security or the rights of property; and have in general been as short in their lives as they have been violent in their deaths. Theoretic politicians, who have patronized this species of

government, have erroneously supposed that by reducing mankind to a perfect equality in their political rights, they would at the same time be perfectly equalized and assimilated in their possessions, their opinions, and their passions.[20]

The Puritans understood the dynamics of small-republic politics. They simply sought to exclude all who might cause trouble. Again, Madison's analysis is instructive: "A religious sect may degenerate into a political faction in a part of the Confederacy; but the variety of sects dispersed over the entire face of it must secure the national councils against any danger from that source."[21]

The rigid New England town structure which helped to organize support for the American Revolution might not have been developed if not for these brutal, even tyrannical, measures. This presents a dilemma for every admirer of the American polity, especially for those who romanticize the local government or the New England-style town meeting.[22] One must view with caution and perhaps suspicion any contemporary calls for a more cohesive American community based on the New England town model. Such calls may betray, at best, a lack of understanding of what formed and sustained those communities. For our part, we must confront the fact that both John Adams and Thomas Jefferson saw the role of the New England town as central to the formation of the republic. These Founders saw strong local government as vital for maintaining free government, and their praise for the New England town should encourage us to reevaluate fundamentally our understanding of local government.

✻ ✻ ✻

1. Alexis de Tocqueville, *Democracy in America*, ed., trans., and intro. Harvey C. Mansfield and Delba Winthrop (Chicago: University of Chicago Press, 2000), 63-64.

2. Cited in Herbert L. Osgood, *The American Colonies in the Eighteenth Century*, vol. 1 (New York: Columbia University Press, 1958), 118.
3. Diana Klebanow, Franklin L. Jonas, and Ira M. Leonard, *Urban Legacy* (New York: Mentor, 1977), 34.
4. Carl Bridenbaugh, *Cities in the Wilderness* (New York: The Ronald Press Co, 1938).
5. Eric H. Monkkonen, *America Becomes Urban: The Development of U.S. Cities and Towns, 1780-1980* (Berkeley: University of California Press, 1988), 57. See also Frederick Jackson Turner, *History, Frontier, and Section: Three Essays* (Albuquerque: University of New Mexico Press, 1993).
6. The tip of lower Manhattan may be an exception, but this layout was abandoned in the early national period as the grid plan was put in place.
7. Monkkonen, *America Becomes Urban*, 54-56. See also William O. Winter, *The Urban Polity* (Toronto: The University of Toronto, 1969), 61.
8. Charles Francis Adams, Jr., *Three Episodes of Massachusetts History* (Boston: Houghton-Mifflin and Co., 1892), 810-812.
9. Herbert Baxter Adams, *The Germanic Origin of New England Towns* (Baltimore: Johns Hopkins University Press, 1882); Herbert Baxter Adams, *Norman Constables in America* (Baltimore: Johns Hopkins University Press, 1883). See also Page P. Smith, *As a City Upon a Hill* (Cambridge: MIT Press, 1973) and Conrad M. Arensberg, "American Communities," *American Anthropologist* 57, no. 6 (1955), 1143-1162.
10. On this point, Herbert Baxter Adams was influenced by his reading of Charles de Secondat, baron de Montesquieu, *The Spirit of the Laws* (1748).
11. Ernest S. Griffith and Charles R. Adrian, *A History of American City Government: The Formation of Traditions, 1775-1870* (Washington D.C.: University Press of America, 1983), 156; and Robert Francis Seybolt, *The Colonial Citizen of New York City* (Madison: University of Wisconsin Press, 1918), 3-4. See also James Wilson, *The Works of James Wilson*, vol. 1, ed. Robert Green McCloskey (Cambridge: The Belknap Press of the Harvard University Press, 1967), 437.
12. Wilson, *Works*, vol. 2, 448-449, 461; George Bryan, "The Genuine Principles of the Ancient Saxon, or English, Constitution," in *American Political Writing during the Founding Era*, vol. 1, eds. Charles S. Hyneman and Donald S. Lutz (Indianapolis: Liberty Press, 1983), 343, 349-352.

13. Turner, *History, Frontier, and Section*.

14. Stanley Elkins and Eric McKitrick, "A Meaning for Turner's Frontier: Part I: Democracy in the Old Northwest," *Political Science Quarterly* 69, no. 3 (1954), 321-322; Stanley Elkins and Eric McKitrick, "A Meaning for Turner's Frontier: Part II: The Southwest Frontier and New England," *Political Science Quarterly* 69, no. 4 (1954), 602.

15. Elkins and McKitrick, "Turner's Frontier: Part I," 322. See also Perry Miller, *The New England Mind: From Colony to Province* (Cambridge: Harvard University Press, 1962) and Perry Miller, *The New England Mind: The Seventeenth Century* (Cambridge: Harvard University Press, 1963).

16. See Smith, *As a City Upon a Hill*. There is some dispute as to the relationship between Calvinist and Lockean influences on American political life. See Thomas G. West, "Transformation of Protestant Theology as a Condition of the American Revolution," and Michael P. Zuckert, "Natural Rights and Protestant Politics," in *Protestantism and the American Founding*, eds. Thomas S. Engeman and Michael P. Zuckert (Notre Dame: University of Notre Dame Press, 2004), 21-76. It may indeed be the case that Lockean philosophy influenced Calvinism more than we appreciate, thus further clarifying Locke's influence on the American regime.

17. Smith, *As a City Upon a Hill*, 112.

18. Michael Zuckerman, *Peaceable Kingdoms: New England Towns in the Eighteenth Century* (New York: Alfred A Knopf, 1970).

19. Parris N. Glendenning and Mavis Mann Reeves, *Pragmatic Federalism: An Intergovernmental View of American Government* (Pacific Palisades, CA: Palisades, 1984), 295.

20. Alexander Hamilton, James Madison, and John Jay, *The Federalist Papers*, ed. Clinton Rossiter, with introduction and notes by Charles Kesler (New York: Mentor, 1999), 49.

21. *The Federalist*, 52.

22. Carla Gardina Pestana, "The Quaker Executions as Myth and History," *The Journal of American History* 80 (1993), 445. See also Miller, *New England Mind: From Colony to Province*; and Miller, *New England Mind: The Seventeenth Century*.

Chapter One

THE COLONIES OF NEW ENGLAND

At the conclusion of his three-volume work *A Defence of the Constitutions*, John Adams encouraged his readers to remember the New England town as one of the most significant contributors to the success of the American Revolution.[1] Given their special role in fostering resistance to British authority, we are obliged to consider with special care the local institutions of New England, and those of Massachusetts in particular. To understand the proper form and structure of local government within the American system, its limitations and virtues, and the Founders' perspectives on the local governments, we need to begin here.

From our discussion of the colonists' expansion into the wilderness, we may derive some fundamental questions about each colonial system. For instance, as the New England population grew, and the frontier expanded, was settlement regulated tightly or loosely? Was the local political structure in the colonies centralized—that is, built around a single source of political authority—or decentralized? Finally, to what extent did each colony's governmental structure permit local government to concern itself with issues larger in scope?

Overview of Local Government in New England

The colony's initial organization was highly centralized. Prior to the Town Act of 1636, colonial authorities declined to recognize towns as entities with any official political status, treating them instead as parts of the single borough of the Massachusetts Bay Colony.[2] The towns around the Massachusetts Bay chafed at such authority, and with the passage of the Town Act, a local control structure began to emerge. Towns were allowed to select their own officers, and town meetings were recognized at all levels within the colony as legitimate.

Contrary to the popular image, settlement of the Massachusetts frontier was highly regulated. Adamant in their desire to avoid the establishment of a plantation economy, the founders of the colony constructed a system of land distribution designed to establish a network of small-scale farms. The key institution in this system was the town, which served as the primary agent of land distribution throughout Massachusetts Bay Colony.[3] In addition to distributive concerns, Massachusetts authorities regulated the creation of the towns out of concerns directly related to colonial security: a scattered array of towns would present greater defense challenges in time of war than a tighter arrangement of settlements.

While the system became more decentralized after the Town Act, the colony continued to regulate closely the lives of its citizens, and the method by which new towns were created as the population grew. Citizens could not travel freely from one town to the next in search of the optimum mix of taxes and services—they could not shop around between towns, so to speak. The towns for their part used their authority to suppress dissenting religious sects, understood as vital for local homogeneity and the strength of the community. The creation of a decentralized structure, in and of itself, proved insufficient for the protection of individual natural rights.

The new Charter of 1691 recognized towns as full corporations, thus further decentralizing the local system. On the other hand, the new charter broadened religious liberty in Massachusetts, protecting the rights of all Protestants, whether Puritan or otherwise, to participate in the political system. This was a significant change in Massachusetts towns respecting the method by which their communities would be sustained, and one must note that both measures were implemented from above. This example provides a lesson applicable to the present day: in protecting local liberty, it may be just as important for those affected by these decisions to monitor and gain influence in levels of government beyond the local.[4]

Like their modern counterparts, most colonial town residents were not intimately involved with day-to-day affairs. Town meetings were held infrequently and attendance was not always good. Yet the structure of local government worked well for extended periods, without intense citizen participation. This is because local government was supplemented, in effect, by representation of the towns as towns in the colonial legislature. Deputies to the colonial assembly actually represented the towns rather than simply the residents of amorphous legislative districts. The residents of the towns thus had reasonable assurance that local concerns were receiving attention at the seat of colonial government. Town representation within the legislature provided Massachusetts residents with an effective form of local government that would neither alienate nor exhaust them.[5]

With respect to the settlement of new towns in the wilderness, Connecticut and Rhode Island followed the example set by Massachusetts, with both colonial governments closely regulating the establishment of new towns. But in both cases another factor bore a heavy influence on the political form and character of new towns in these colonies, namely the threat of war. Connecticut hastened the establishment of a strong local system in the face of the Pequot War (1637).[6] Several decades later, Rhode Island faced significant early challenges to its municipal poor relief structure due to the devastating impact of King Phillip's War (1675-1676). As for the structure of the two colonies' town systems, both were largely decentralized. Although the colonial government of Connecticut retained the authority to approve new towns, Connecticut town representatives had a direct hand in crafting the colony's framing document, the Fundamental Orders of 1639.[7] In addition, as was the case in Massachusetts, towns acted as the unit of representation in the colonial assembly. This gave towns direct input into decisions at the colonial level.

As for Rhode Island, its towns enjoyed a greater degree of authority than those of either Massachusetts or Connecticut. Prior to the Charter of 1663, Rhode Island town governments wielded the power to nullify existing colonial legislation, or directly initiate new colonial laws. These practices ended with the enactment of the new charter. The town deputies in the colonial assembly, however, still retained the balance of power in Rhode Island politics.

In some respects, then, Connecticut and Rhode Island were more decentralized than Massachusetts. Rhode Island may have had the most permissive environment for religious freedom among the New England colonies. But neither the local system of Connecticut nor Rhode Island was a free market of town residence. The entry barriers to such a "market" were still significant. Even though religious standards were much looser in Connecticut and virtually non-existent in Rhode Island, those without solid character references and without sufficient means to sustain themselves found it difficult to obtain legal residence in a town.

Attendance at town meetings in Connecticut and Rhode Island was frequently poor.[8] As was the case with Massachusetts, this may have reflected the reality that towns were politically strong vis-à-vis the colonial government.[9] In Connecticut and Rhode Island, the lack of attention to local affairs may have served as an implicit endorsement of the manner in which colonial politics were conducted. After all, Connecticut and Rhode Island had been granted high degrees of autonomy by the British Crown.

In what follows, we take a more detailed look at the New England colonies and the specifics of their local government. Our central question concerns the extent to which the region's governance required significant citizen participation, or whether the relatively organized structure of local government allowed communities to mobilize in the event of a crisis.

Massachusetts

Town Government

Colonial North Americans brought the traditions of class status with them from the Old World, and residents of the colonial Massachusetts town were classified as proprietors, freemen, and inhabitants. Those without official status were disallowed from holding office, or from establishing permanent residence in a town. Strangers were likely to receive an official notification from the town constable that their presence was illegal and that they should make immediate plans to depart. Those who failed to leave could receive a fine, corporal punishment, or, in the case of officially sanctioned heretics, a capital sentence.

The *proprietors* consisted of those original town settlers who had successfully applied to the colonial legislature for the establishment of a new town. These were the individuals who had framed the original town covenant and divided town lands into farm plots, house lots, common meadows, and common woodlands. While private farm and house plots were owned outright on a fee-simple basis, the proprietors retained authority to make subsequent decisions about the conversion of common land to private holdings.

The status of *freeman* entitled one to hold colonial offices and vote in elections for town deputies to the legislature. A freeman was a male of good estate—that is to say, a property owner—who counted himself a follower of orthodox Puritan doctrine, though this latter obligation was liberalized with the Charter of 1691. With respect to voting rights in the town meeting, freemen enjoyed a status equal to the proprietors.

An *inhabitant*, by contrast, was a person who had been officially sanctioned by the town to own land and participate in local decisions, yet did not hold enough property to qualify for the colony-wide status of freeman. Those desiring to settle in a town had first to be approved as inhabitants in a town meeting. Prospective inhabitants were required to demonstrate that they had the means to maintain themselves and, therefore, would not become a burden on the town treasury. Applicants were also required to provide character references from the previous town in which they lived. And—in the years before the 1691 Charter—new inhabitants were required to accept the orthodox interpretation of Calvinist Protestantism then accepted in the Massachusetts colony or quietly submit to paying the taxes necessary for the support of an orthodox minister in the town. This religious requirement had been vital to the homogeneity of Puritan communities during the Antinomian

Crisis (1636-1638) and the Quaker troubles (1656-1661).[10] Once approved, inhabitants could regularly participate in the town meeting and vote on town measures.[11] Inhabitants, however, were not permitted to vote in elections for town deputies.[12] While these restrictions will no doubt appear illiberal to modern notions of equality, Puritan town government was arguably one of the more democratic institutions at that point in history. For example, from the town records of Dedham in 1647, Kenneth Lockridge calculates that 70 percent of the town was officially eligible to vote in the town meeting. By 1666, that number reached 91 percent. By 1670, however, with the property requirement set at £80, only 25 percent were officially eligible. With the implementation of the 1691 Charter, however, the property requirement for a freehold was cut in half, thus restoring wider eligibility.[13] "Nowhere in the entire world," writes Carl Bridenbaugh in *Cities in Revolt*, "did so large a number of the populace participate in the government of their city as elected officials."[14]

The periodic meeting of town residents was the most important political institution in Massachusetts, and they were held frequently in the newly established towns. In her examination of colonial town records, historian Anne Bush Maclear learned that Cambridge, founded in 1630, began holding meetings "every second Monday" in 1632, with neighboring Dorchester holding a weekly "general meeting of the inhabitants of the plantation at the meeting house" every Monday beginning in 1633.[15] This pattern was followed throughout the region, with the frequency of town meetings dropping to a few times each year as the town matured over the next century.[16] In New England today, town meetings are typically limited to an annual meeting at which budget approval is the central item of business, and such special meetings as are called throughout the year.

As for town democracy, a warrant for a town meeting would be cried out by the constable or designated town official.[17] Notices could also be placed on town signposts, with the warrant stating the time and purpose of the meeting. Attendance at town meetings was mandatory, with fines imposed for absence or tardiness.[18] The frequent application of such fines would indicate that poor attendance was a recurring problem.[19] Once assembled, the town meeting selected a moderator as its first order of business, responsible for maintaining the general order of the meeting.[20] The moderator acted as a speaker of the town meeting and was responsible for keeping the meeting's business within the confines of the agenda, and held the authority to determine who could be recognized to speak or vote.[21] Colonial scholar John Sly contends that meeting procedures could be quite irregular and that the participation rules may have been loosely enforced, allowing for broader participation than official standards might indicate.[22] Robert E. Brown concludes that there was, in practice, wide latitude granted to the moderator in determining a person's eligibility to vote in a town meeting, noting that even if a person were excluded from voting, his right to deliberate was recognized.[23]

Those in attendance gathered in the meeting house, which was also the site of weekly church services. As was the case with Sabbath worship, seating was assigned at a town meeting, with a seat's location corresponding to one's status in the community.[24] Benches for men and women were placed on opposite sides of the meeting house, just as they were during regular worship services.[25] Fines were sometimes levied on those who stood on their seats in order to gain a better view.[26]

From her detailed analysis of Hadley town records, Ellen Callahan offers further insight into the Massachusetts town meeting.[27] Once the meeting was underway and operating according to the authority of the moderator, no one was permitted to leave, under pain of fine, without permission. The meetings could at times be raucous, and there appear in the Hadley records instances in which individuals, unwilling to abide by meeting protocol, were forcibly removed from the meeting house. The warrant for the meeting would then be read by the town clerk, typically having been written by the town selectmen, annually elected officers who acted as a city council. Once the warrant was read and seconded, the town pastor offered up a prayer, and with that, the floor would be open for motions as to the taking up of additional agenda items. Such motions required a second. Once a motion was recognized, the moderator would put the issue to a vote. Votes could be cast in one of three ways: *viva voce* (by voice), by division, or by "kernel." If the vote were to be made by voice, the moderator determined the outcome. If the result was hard to determine, the moderator could call for a division of the ayes and nays. Charles Francis Adams found evidence that those voting aye moved to the women's side of the meeting house while those voting nay stood on the men's side, with an appointed teller determining the outcome.[28] As for the still more precise kernel method, John Sly discovered that those voting aye placed a wheat kernel in front of the teller or other designated official, while those voting nay placed a corn kernel.[29] The kernels would then be divided and counted to determine the result. A clerk would keep a record of the meeting, noting the issues involved and, at times, opinions dissenting from the majority.[30]

Land use tended to be a commonplace issue before a town meeting, as were church affairs, school matters, and expenses relating to poor relief. Records from Braintree indicate that secession efforts by those wishing to form a new town were frequent as well.[31] According to the Braintree records analyzed by Charles Francis Adams and those of several other towns reviewed by historian Michael Zuckerman, agenda items also included appointment of officers, economic regulations, taxes, military matters, disease epidemics, quarrels within the community, admission of new members, relations with other towns, Indian affairs, colonial matters, relations with the Crown, religious heresies, highways, bridges, care for the insane, currency matters, and public debt.[32]

Town Officers

The most important Massachusetts town officers were the selectmen, charged with maintaining the regular administration of affairs and setting the prices for commodities and labor.[33] These officers were chosen annually in a town meeting and could act in the name of the town, subject to review by the town meeting.[34] In addition, the selectmen could act as a trial court for minor offenses.[35] There were no term limits for this office.[36] In the seventeenth century, selectmen, most often consisting of the town's elite, could count on a lifetime of service, perhaps rotating terms of service within a small clique.[37] From the town records of Dedham, however, there is evidence that turnover increased in the eighteenth century, with a wider group serving in office.[38]

In addition to the selectmen, the major officers in a given town included the *clerk, commissioner, constable, tithingman, fence-viewer,* and *surveyor of highways.*[39] The *clerk* recorded births and deaths and gave notice of a court summons in civil cases.[40] The *commissioner* was a local magistrate who also served as the town tax assessor.[41] A *constable* was in charge of maintaining order in a town and would also, periodically, announce town meetings and warn-out strangers. The responsibilities of a *tithingman* included maintaining order at town meetings—acting, for all intents and purposes, as a sergeant-at-arms. In addition, the tithingman would also be in charge of ensuring regular Sunday worship and the enforcement of laws designed to maintain the town's moral climate. A *fence-viewer* was selected to inspect fences on private and common land to help prevent the escape of herd animals. Such wandering beasts could cause crop damage and other hazards to property. The *surveyor of highways* was responsible for the maintenance and planning of a road system in a given town, including bridges and other infrastructure. The surveyor of highways could compel residents to perform work on the roads.[42]

Table 1.1 Town Officers in Massachusetts

Selectman	Pound-Keeper	Rater (taxes)
Clerk	Drummer	Sealer of Leather
Moderator	Clerk of the Market	Water Bailiff
Commissioner	Perambulator	Procurer of Wood
Constable	Overseer of Fences	Town Meeting Clerk
Tithingman	Bell Ringer	Delinquency Judge
Grave Digger	Surveyor of Highways	Meat Packer
Fence-Viewer	Fish Packer	Shepherd
Treasurer	Hog Reeve	Field Driver
Night Watchman	Goat Reeve	Sexton

Sources: Carl Bridenbaugh, *Cities in the Wilderness* (New York: The Ronald Press Co., 1938), 165; Charles Francis Adams, Jr., *Three Episodes of Massachusetts History* (Boston: Houghton-Mifflin and Co., 1892), 819-820; Ellen Elizabeth Callahan, *Hadley: A Study of the Political Development of a Typical New England Town from the Official Records, 1659-1930* (Northampton, MA: Department of History, Smith College, 1931), 22, 26; Blake McKelvey, *The City in American History* (London: Allen and Unwin, 1969),18; John Farifield Sly, *Town Government in Massachusetts* (Hamden, CT: Archon Books, 1967), 39, 40, 50.

It is doubtful that the typical town residents relished being appointed to a town office, most of which were unpaid. Many were also unpleasant, especially the law-enforcement responsibilities associated with the office of constable. Accordingly, Charles Francis Adams notes that fines from those who decline to accept a town position provided a reliable source of town funds. Robert D. Brown argues that the routine selection of a town's elite to important public offices was itself a sign of a town's democracy. Many of these offices were unpleasant and carried a potential financial burden for the official, such that office-holding, writes Carl Bridenbaugh, amounted to "a form of taxation based on wealth, and men of small means were content to divide the lesser burdens of office among themselves, designating those of greater wealth and higher status to carry the larger public load."[43]

Town Finance

A Massachusetts town would select an official to compile the tax list, from which the town constable would collect taxes.[44] The parish deacon would perform the same duty for church taxes.[45] The constable was held personally responsible for the collection of taxes, and any deficiency in the amount collected would have to be remedied from the constable's own financial resources. Tax collection, therefore, was a financially risky endeavor for the constable. In Chapter Three we will see that John Adams warned ambitious young men about the dangers of holding the office of constable. Given the harm that could come to a household's finances, town members were expected to rotate this office among themselves, thus sharing its burdens.[46]

There was originally nothing like the modern budget system with which we are today familiar. Expenditures were met in an ad hoc fashion.[47] By the late seventeenth century, however, local finance in Massachusetts had taken on a more regular form. The annual needs of the town began to be listed in advance and the town tax rate was set accordingly. With the adoption of a budget system, selectmen became more actively and directly involved in the town's financial affairs vis-à-vis the town meeting.[48]

Table 1.2. British Currency Denominations

1 Gold Guinea = £1 1s = 21s = 252d

1 Gold Sovereign = £1 = 20s = 240d

1 Pound = £1 = 20s = 240d

1 Mark = 13s4d = 160d

1 Crown = 5s = 60d

1 Shilling = 1s = 12d

1 Sixpence = 6d

1 Threepence = 3d

1 Penny = 1d

1 Halfpence = 1/2d = 2 farthings

1 Farthing = 1/4d

Source: Department of Special Collections, University of Notre Dame Libraries < http://www.coins.nd.edu/ColCoin/ColCoinIntros/BritishDenominations1.html > (Accessed 8 August 2004).

The town was not only responsible for collecting the town rate, but also the county and colony-wide rates as well. These rates were to be paid by all residents, freeman and non-freeman alike. A single "rate" was 1d (penny) per £1 of visible estate. Several rates could be collected at one time by each taxing entity. A rate could be paid in staples or in currency, with the ratio of staples to currency payments often set in advance.[49]

The number of rates collected depended upon the needs of each level of government. For example, expenditures during wartime would be quite high to supply troops with *matériel*. War also strained the welfare systems of towns, and colonial wars resulted in scores of disabled veterans, not to mention widows and orphans entitled to relief by the towns.[50] Care for the poor and disabled was a prominent feature in town appropriations. As Charles Francis Adams notes, "Everyone had a right to insist on being kept from starving and freezing."[51] Adams offers the following list of annual appropriations from the 1694 town records of Braintree:

£5 30s: John Belsher's widow's maintenance

30s: Thomas Revill for keeping William Dimblebee

25s: ringing the bell and sweeping the meeting house

8s: mending the town pound

7s: William Savill for Dimblebee's coffin

8s: constables for warning the town

5s: for the exchange of a town cow to Samuel Speer

10s: Thomas Bas for ringing the bell formerly

Courts

From its earliest days, the local judicial system in colonial Massachusetts was connected to colonial government. Massachusetts town officials, the selectmen, were originally allowed to try minor offenses against town ordinances. But in 1638, the judicial role of the selectmen was supplemented by the creation of the office of commissioner, nominated by the town and confirmed by final approval of the colonial government. These commissioners were limited to deciding cases involving smaller sums under 20 shillings; that amount increased over time to 40 shillings.[52] The Massachusetts colonial legislature created another local judicial office in 1641, the town clerk who, like the commissioners, was nominated within a town, but received his official commission from the colony. The clerk issued court summonses and kept vital town records.[53] In addition, a colonial assistant was empowered to try cases in his hometown.[54] As for the county courts, they handled a wide variety of issues, including some that would be described today as regulation.[55]

With enactment of the Charter of 1691, the county courts were split into two bodies, one for civil cases and another for criminal ones.[56] More serious cases were heard by the colonial assistants who sat as a court. In addition to their original jurisdiction in felonies, the court of assistants had appellate jurisdiction.[57] Massachusetts also had a jury system.[58] Juries could include members from towns other than the one in which the case was tried in order to enhance impartiality.[59]

Education

The maintenance of a public school system was a major town responsibility. It was also a major expenditure. By the end of the seventeenth century, colonial Boston was apportioning nearly half its annual expenditures to education.[60] Public schools were governed by the town meeting and administered by the selectmen, and required frequent attention.[61] Anne Maclear reports that the choice of schoolmaster, his salary, the location and maintenance of the schoolhouse, and the curriculum were all decisions made in town meetings, with selectmen handling the day-to-day affairs of town schools.[62] Schools were supported in a variety of ways. In the case of Braintree, we know that rental payments made for the use of town land helped to support local schools, supplemented by the town's sale of firewood to Boston, and the town rate and tuition payments.[63] Tuition was often a feature of Massachusetts colonial public education, with Braintree's tuition of 1 shilling per academic quarter in

1700, and the following year 5 shillings per annum as typical.[64] Provisions existed, however, for those unable to pay.[65] In Watertown, for example, as of 1667, a public education was available to inhabitants without charge.[66] As is the case today with out-state residents attending state universities, pupils attending school other than their normal residence could expect to pay higher tuition.[67] In Braintree, a non-resident could expect to pay four times the five shillings per annum tuition.[68]

Faculty of the public schools received a salary somewhat less than clergy. The schoolmaster of Braintree was awarded a salary of £30 in 1679, with the figure rising to £34 by 1720, about one-third of that for the town minister.[69] The schoolmaster received significant fringe benefits, however, including exemption from militia service and from colonial taxes.[70] Public schools followed the English education model, and the town of Braintree supported a grammar school for the youngest students and a Latin school.[71] Boston boasted five public schools, including the renowned Boston Latin School, the nation's oldest public education establishment.[72] In addition to support for local public schools, the towns provided ancillary support to the colony's higher education. The 1669 town expenditure of Braintree for the support of the colonial college fund was £87 14s 6d, a considerable sum, nearly three times the level of support for the town schoolmaster and nearly equal to the town minister's salary.[73]

Education responsibilities for the colonial townsfolk did not stop with financial support. Parents were expected to ensure that their children were able to master basic academic skills. The Massachusetts legislature enacted a law in 1735 requiring that children failing to master the alphabet by age six would be placed with another family with the hope that they would receive proper instruction.[74]

Plymouth

First settled in 1620, Plymouth existed as an independent colony until 1691 when it was joined with Massachusetts under the new charter imposed by the Crown, at which time the full name became "Massachusetts and Plymouth Colonies."[75] In the beginning, land in the Plymouth colony was held and farmed communally, but harvests were so poor that the plan was abandoned beginning in 1623 and finally in 1627 as a complete failure.[76]

As for the political structure of the colony, the signers of the Mayflower Compact sat as a legislature with plenary power. Acting in this capacity, the body held annual sessions, choosing a governor and a captain (chief military officer) who would each serve one-year terms. The colonial government set town boundaries and also, during the first decade of settlement, appointed town officers.

Beginning in 1630, the colonial authorities allowed each town to manage its daily affairs and to choose its own selectmen, constables, and surveyors of highways, each subject to approval by the legislature. In 1636, the very year the Massachusetts Bay Colony would do the same, Plymouth allowed for town representation in the legislature with two from each town, save for the town of Plymouth, which was apportioned five representatives. The towns were further grouped into three counties in 1685. The counties were to serve as units of judicial administration whose officials would be appointed by the legislature.[77]

New Hampshire

New Hampshire was granted status as a colony independent from Massachusetts in 1680. Until 1682, when a royal lieutenant governor was installed, New Hampshire was governed by a president, deputy president, council and an assembly. The president was appointed by the Crown. The land system was similar to that in Massachusetts. New Hampshire's citizens elected assembly members annually, and had a regular court system, with the legislature serving as a court of appeal, also similar to Massachusetts. Those of good estate, of the Protestant faith, who took an oath of allegiance to the Crown could vote in New Hampshire.[78] Like its parent to the south, the New Hampshire colonial government primarily concerned itself with the formation of new towns, town boundaries, and the creation of new parishes.[79]

Connecticut

The system of local government in Connecticut bore many similarities to the one which took root in Massachusetts. Connecticut separated from Massachusetts in 1635, with its founders establishing the *Fundamental Orders*, a document long regarded as the first written constitution, and one establishing the Congregational Church as the new entity's recognized religious body. Under the *Fundamental Orders*, Connecticut's citizens agreed to abide by the decisions of a unicameral legislative body, the General Court, a political system that remained in place until the *Fundamental Orders* was replaced by the Connecticut Charter in 1662. Even after 1698 when the General Court was divided to become the two-house General Assembly, the legislature enjoyed more authority than either the colony's executive or judiciary. Suffrage was granted any adult freeman owning taxable property valued at 40 shillings.

Town Government

Like Massachusetts, the central political organization of Connecticut local government was the town meeting.[80] According to historian Bruce Daniels, property requirements for participating in town meetings were low, ensuring virtual universal white male participation on local matters. Any legal resident with property valued at more than 50s (£2 10s) could participate. This figure was drastically lower than that for Massachusetts, whose requirement for local participation was set at £20 for most of the colonial period. On the other hand, like Massachusetts, residency in Connecticut towns was limited to those of good moral standing and able to supply the requisite character references.[81]

While formal requirements for participation in Connecticut local affairs were loose by colonial standards, the practical standards were looser still. Historian Charles Andrews, in his study of Connecticut local government, contends that towns resisted the very idea of restrictions on town voting. As evidence of this, colonial records include warnings issued to towns respecting participation of sojourners in town meetings. This indicates that the concerned inhabitant, legal or not, or perhaps even the town crank, enjoyed a voice in a town meeting from time to time.[82] But the open character of the Connecticut town meeting was less likely due to inherent Yankee liberality than a display of strength by the Connecticut Puritans, whose authority by virtue of their predominance was never in question. Herbert Osgood argues that Connecticut's populace was so homogenous that town meetings, by and large, were quiet affairs. Controversies occurred infrequently and officers were routinely returned to the same office.[83] One modern observer goes so far as to describe Connecticut as a stable "deference democracy."[84]

Connecticut Calvinists appear to have been devoted to the orderly conduct of affairs but could tolerate flexibility in procedure due to the knowledge that a favorable outcome was inevitable.[85] The easygoing spirit of Connecticut town government is captured succinctly by Charles Andrews:

"Absence from town meeting was not uncommon, from worship rare."[86]

Town Officers and Functions

The colonial-era Connecticut town was endowed with most of the powers one associates with modern day cities.[87] Towns controlled the allocation and regulation of lands within their boundaries, and could select their own officers, impose sanctions for minor criminal and civil violations, and could impose local taxes.[88] Town officers in Connecticut were chosen by ballot at a town meeting.[89] While there was significant turnover from year-to-year for middle-level offices, higher positions within a town were routinely held by a small cadre of a town's elite.[90] The names and duties of town officers were similar to those in Massachusetts.[91]

Connecticut's land allocation system was also similar to that of Massachusetts. The original proprietors of Connecticut towns, however, took greater advantage of their position than those in Massachusetts Bay Colony, allocating to themselves the choicest of plots.[92]

Road construction and maintenance was a primary function of town government. According to Richard Bushman, the towns held eminent domain power with respect to the building of roads.[93] To that effect, the surveyor of highways could commandeer labor from town residents, with a 5 shilling fine imposed on those failing to report.[94] Towns were also held responsible for the education of their children. In 1700, the legislature created a school commission, similar in scope and function to the modern school board.[95] As the seventeenth century drew to a close, Connecticut towns increasingly faced the issue of town secession, a major issue in Massachusetts as well.

As a town's population spread out from the village center,

disputes were known to have developed over the location of the meeting house and the construction of new roads.[96] At first, such difficulties were settled by granting those living at a certain distance from the meeting house—usually 5 or 6 miles—an exemption from attending the original meeting house for worship.[97] These "outlivers" were granted the authority to build and support a winter meeting house. When this proved inadequate, those in outlying districts could then request that the legislature create a new town. But this procedure was often controversial, requiring as it did that the original town would lose a significant portion of its tax base.[98] This process of "hiving-off" was how most new towns were formed in Connecticut.[99]

Counties

In addition to the functions performed by towns, counties in Connecticut rose in prominence with the creation of county courts in 1666. Along with their judicial responsibilities, county governments were responsible for deploying troops and collecting taxes, with a county assessor taking over this duty from the selectmen in 1704.[100]

The typical county court comprised a presiding judge assisted by three justices of the peace. The justices in Connecticut lacked the executive authority held by their counterparts in other colonies; a justice of the peace in Connecticut was, according to Bruce Daniels, a strictly judicial official.[101] County justices had great demands placed upon them by Connecticut's litigious residents. According to Daniels, the heavy civil caseload suggests that "colonial men sued one another at the drop of a hat."[102] Another important local official was the county sheriff, primarily responsible for serving warrants, a function which exists to this day in Connecticut.[103]

The chief trial court for the colony's most serious cases was the Court of Assistants, comprising at least seven of the colony's twelve assistants, and assembled to hear all cases involving capital punishment or banishment. This court was replaced by the Superior Court in 1711, with the responsibilities transferred to regular justices. Appeals from the Superior Court or Court of Assistants could be heard by the legislature.[104]

Rhode Island

Originating from the actions of religious dissenters Roger Williams and Anne Hutchinson in the 1630s, Rhode Island and Providence Plantations received a royal Charter in 1663 from Charles II. That document specified a General Assembly and governmental system to such a degree that it served as the Rhode Island constitution until 1842. Voting was limited to property owners.

Town Government

Rhode Island was a federation of towns to an extent greater even than Massachusetts.[105] Towns were keen to guard their authority to act in local affairs and, for the most part, the General Assembly respected town authority.[106] The core of town power in Rhode Island, as was the case in all of New England, was the town meeting. And, while the percentage of voting citizens participating in town meetings was routinely low, historian Bruce C. Daniels reports that, "although not more than 30 percent of the adult males went to even highly attended meetings, the number could be fairly high."[107]

Voter turnout, however, for elections was higher in Rhode Island than in Connecticut, the colony that had a system most similar to that of Rhode Island.[108] It is possible that poor attendance at town meetings could be accounted for by the higher frequency of town meetings in Rhode Island, or to the widespread belief that the colonial government was truly under the control of the towns via their deputies in the General Assembly.[109] Professor Daniels describes the Rhode Island system as a mixture of apathy and highly participatory democracy.[110]

Rhode Island's town meetings were conducted in a manner similar to that in other New England colonies and were concerned with similar agenda items, save the religious controversies that afflicted Massachusetts and Connecticut in the seventeenth century. The selectmen or "council" were chosen at the meeting and given authority to administer the day-to-day affairs of a town.

In addition to the use of the word "council," other modern features of Rhode Island government were its comparatively greater reliance upon paid officials and its relatively detailed record-keeping. The administrative officers in the Rhode Island town were similar to those in other colonies: clerk, treasurer, constable, fence-viewer, surveyor of highway, constables, etc.[111] Because of Rhode Island's unique standard of church and state separation, no tithingmen were appointed to regulate religious conduct.[112]

The town surveyor of highways could compel residents to provide labor for the building and maintenance of town roads. Carl Bridenbaugh finds evidence from the Newport town records that such labor was required of residents for three days to build and repair roads in the outlying "woods" part of the town.[113] In 1715, the General Assembly further enhanced the road-building authority of the town by granting it eminent domain power. However, unlike the cavalier standards applied by many towns today with respect to the taking of property for "public use," a town jury was impaneled to assess the validity of the town's claim.[114] Poor relief was also an important responsibility of the Rhode Island town, one that could stretch the limits of town finance.[115] In addition, among other responsibilities, the town regulated economic activity, was responsible for public health measures, and helped create firefighting companies.[116]

Finance

Education was, in part, the responsibility of the town, but poor relief was the predominant budget item in Rhode Island town finance. According to the town records of Scituate, Rhode Island, poor relief accounted for 55 percent of town expenditures from 1763 to 1765. This amount nearly doubles that spent for the second-most prominent item, salaries for tax collectors.[117] In addition to the increase that would occur during times of economic depression, poverty levels rose during periods of warfare. Displaced family members and those whose primary providers had been casualties either flocked to the towns or were stranded as indigents on outlying farms.

While poor relief in the seventeenth century took the form of direct payments or subsidies to those private residents who provided care for the poor, such assistance became more institutionalized in the eighteenth century.[118] Almshouses and workhouses became a more regular feature of indigent care. For example, Newport constructed an almshouse in 1716 and several workhouses in the 1720s. In addition, proceeds from a lottery were used to fund construction of an additional workhouse in 1769.[119] To limit their financial liability, towns were eager to keep out those who might become public charges. Towns were empowered to deny residency to anyone unless they first provided a bond, thus protecting the town against any charges that may result from potential indigence.[120] Those asked to leave a town were warned not to return under pain of corporal punishment. Bruce Daniels offers the following insight:

> The councils were allowed to require a bond from any person to leave the town, or they could reject any prospective inhabitant. If a person refused to post a bond or leave town, the council could apply to a justice of the peace for warrant and fine the person five pounds or administer a whipping not to exceed twenty stripes.[121]

And, as Daniels continues, Rhode Islanders would indeed follow through on these threats:

> Nor was the whipping symbolic. Usually it was "ten stripes upon the naked back," but a woman returning to Portsmouth was whipped fifteen stripes and two women in Providence were whipped fifteen and twenty stripes respectively.[122]

As an additional deterrent to a person seeking public assistance, those receiving poor relief were required to wear badges identifying them as indigent.[123]

To pay for poor relief and other public expenses, Rhode Island towns could levy taxes without the need to seek colonial permission.[124] But permission is one thing, and collection another: town officials were hard pressed to collect sufficient tax monies to meet town expenditures. The resistance to both rate-setting and collection came from both the town meeting and the individuals who were targeted.[125] Such resistance could take the form of a town meeting refusing to set rates necessary to cover expenditures, or in the form of individual lawsuits directed at tax collectors.[126]

The situation could be precarious for town treasurers and assessors who were personally responsible for the amount of money collected and would be liable for any debts incurred due to a lack of public funds. It will hardly be surprising to find that local tax officials also filed lawsuits to recover losses.[127] Other sources of income included town lotteries and duties paid on imported slaves.[128]

Conclusion

The decentralized yet highly structured system of local government in the New England colonies allowed for an effective provision of important services, including firefighting, education, and poor relief, especially as compared to its sister colonies to the south. The towns, for the most part, were also effective in organizing militia during times of public danger. Furthermore, it was the New England town governments that led the colonial resistance to James II in the 1680s and against George III in the years leading to the Revolution.

The principal unit of local government in the colonies that comprised New England was the town. The most important institution in the town was the town meeting. The primary officers in the town were the selectmen, a body that was the rough equivalent of the modern city council.[129] Particular responsibilities were handled by town officers, most notably the town clerk, constable, surveyor of highways, tithingman, and fence-viewer. With the creation of counties, sheriffs served to assist the courts and to collect taxes. Similar positions were created by all colonial local governments. In this respect, at least, there is little difference in the structure of local governments between the New England colonies, middle colonies, and southern colonies. In New England, these and other colonial functions were funded primarily through property taxes, which in Massachusetts could be particularly high. Property tax revenues were supplemented by poll taxes, import duties, export duties, and excise taxes.

✸ ✸ ✸

1. In the Postscript to this work, a letter to the Abbé de Mably, Adams writes: "Permit me, sir, before I finish this letter, to point at a key to all this history. There is a general analogy in the governments and characters of all the thirteen states; but it was not till the debates and the war began in Massachusetts Bay, the principal province of New England, that their primitive institutions produced their first effect." John Adams, *A Defence of the Constitutions of Government of the United States of America* (1807), as reprinted in *The Works of John Adams* (Boston: Little, Brown and Company, 1851), vol. 5, 494.

2. Kenneth A. Lockridge, *A New England Town: The First Hundred Years* (New York: W.W. Norton and Company, 1985), 38.

3. Edward Channing, *Town and County Government in the English Colonies of North America* (Baltimore: Johns Hopkins University Press, 1884), 24; Sam Bass Warner, Jr., *The Urban Wilderness* (New York: Harper and Row Publishers, 1972), 9.

4. Benjamin Woods Labaree, *Colonial Massachusetts: A History* (Millwood, NY: KTO Press, 1979), 119. See also Herbert Osgood, *The American Colonies in the Seventeenth Century*, vol. 1, 410, 441.

5. Robert Eldon Brown, *Middle-Class Democracy and the Revolution in Massachusetts, 1691-1780* (Ithaca, NY: Cornell University Press, 1955), 78.

6. Osgood, *Seventeenth Century*, vol. 1, 305-306. See also Robert J. Taylor, *Colonial Connecticut: A History* (Millwood, NY: KTO Press, 1979), 13-15.

7. Charles McLean Andrews, *The River Towns of Connecticut* (Baltimore: Johns Hopkins University Press, 1889), 36.

8. Bruce C. Daniels, *Dissent and Conformity on Narragansett Bay* (Middletown, CT: Wesleyan University Press, 1983), 98. Furthermore, as Daniels notes, the poor turnout for town meetings was not due to lack of effort on the part of town officials to ensure good attendance. *Dissent*, 99.

9. Andrews, *River Towns*, 78.

10. Ellen Elizabeth Callahan, *Hadley: A Study of the Political Development of a Typical New England Town from the Official Records 1659-1930* (Northampton, MA: Department of History of Smith College, 1931), 15; Kenneth A. Lockridge, *A New England Town*, 8; Anne Bush Maclear, *Early New England Towns: A Comparative Study of Their Development* (New York: AMS Press, 1967), 132-135; John F. Sly, *Town Government in Massachusetts, 1620-1930* (Hamden, CT: Archon Books, 1967), 45-48.

11. Callahan, *Hadley*, 15.

12. Citing evidence from as early as 1647, John Sly notes that inhabitants could participate in town decisions as long as freemen constituted a majority of those present. Sly, *Town Government*, 47-48.
13. Lockridge, *A New England Town*, 49, 129.
14. Carl Bridenbaugh, *Cities in Revolt* (New York: Alfred A. Knopf, 1955), 6.
15. Maclear, *Early New England Towns*, 107.
16. Bruce C. Daniels, *The Connecticut Town* (Middletown, CT: Wesleyan University Press, 1979), 81. However, as Daniels notes, the frequency tended to increase during times of crisis. And Boston, for example, retained the town meeting until 1822. See William O. Winter, *State and Local Government in a Decentralized Republic* (New York: Macmillan Publishing Co., 1981), 22.
17. Of course, those required to attend a particular meeting would vary, depending upon whether the scheduled gathering would be a general town meeting, for freemen only, or for the proprietors. Sly, *Town Government*, 50. David Syrett finds that few announcements of a town meeting were made in newspapers and that there were numerous irregularities in the calling of town meetings. David Syrett, "Town Meeting Politics in Massachusetts: 1776-1786," *William and Mary Quarterly* 21, no. 3, 3rd Series (1964), 356-358.
18. Maclear, *Early New England Towns*, 110; Sly, *Town Government*, 43.
19. Syrett, "Town Meeting," 355. Syrett notes that weather and road conditions may have played a factor in poor attendance at town meetings.
20. Callahan, *Hadley*, 16; Maclear, *Early New England Towns*, 111; Sly, *Town Government*, 43.
21. Lockridge, *A New England Town*, 48; Sly, *Town Government*, 43.
22. B. Katherine Brown, "The Controversy over the Franchise in Puritan Massachusetts 1954-1974," *William and Mary Quarterly* 33, no. 2, 3rd Series, (1976), 241; Sly, *Town Government*, 51, 95; Syrett, "Town Meeting," 361. Michael Zuckerman has an interesting hypothesis about the loose standards of determining eligibility to participate in town meetings. It may have been the case that it was simply more convenient to allow broader participation. Zuckerman, "The Social Context of Democracy in Massachusetts," *William and Mary Quarterly* 25, no. 1, 3rd Series (1968), 528.
23. Robert E. Bown, *Middle-Class Democracy*, 99.
24. Lockridge, *A New England Town*, 16.
25. C. F. Adams, *Three Episodes*, 734.

26. Ibid., 743.
27. Callahan, *Hadley*, 17.
28. C. F. Adams, *Three Episodes*, 734.
29. Sly, *Town Government*, 44.
30. C. F. Adams, *Three Episodes*, 820.
31. Ibid., 820-821.
32. Zuckerman, *Peaceable Kingdoms*, 261; C. F. Adams, *Three Episodes*, 812. See also Callahan, *Hadley*, 20.
33. Lockridge, *A New England Town*, 38-40; Callahan, *Hadley*, 23-24; Bridenbaugh, *Cities in the Wilderness*, 24.
34. Channing, *Town and County*, 30.
35. Lockridge, *A New England Town*, 40.
36. Maclear, *Early New England Towns*, 117.
37. Lockridge, *A New England Town*, 43.
38. Ibid., 125.
39. C. F. Adams, *Three Episodes*, 819.
40. Maclear, *Early New England Towns*, 51. The selection of a town clerk was made in a slightly different fashion than other offices. The town would nominate a candidate, who then would have to be approved by the colonial government.
41. Callahan, *Hadley*, 9; Sly, *Town Government*, 39; Osgood, *Seventeenth Century*, vol. 1, 474.
42. Bridenbaugh, *Cities in the Wilderness*, 163.
43. Bridenbaugh, *Revolt*, 7; R. E. Brown, *Middle-Class Democracy*, 98; R. D. Brown, *Revolutionary Politics in Massachusetts* (Cambridge: Harvard University Press), 5.
44. Maclear, *Early New England Towns*, 64-65, 78; C. F. Adams, *Episodes*, 823-824.
45. Maclear, *Early New England Towns*, 68.
46. C. F. Adams, *Episodes*, 824.
47. Maclear, *Early New England Towns*, 55.
48. Ibid., 67-68.
49. Ibid., 72.
50. C. F. Adams, *Episodes*, 589.
51. Ibid., 647.
52. Maclear, *Early New England Towns*, 47. In the long-standing (late

fifteenth century to 1971) British monetary system, the basic units were the pence (abbreviated d.), the shilling (s.), and the pound (£), with 12 pence to the shilling, 20 shillings to the pound, and hence 240 pence to the pound.

53. Osgood, *Seventeenth Century*, vol. 1, 192; Maclear, *Early New England Towns*, 51.
54. Maclear, *Early New England Towns*, 46; Osgood, *Seventeenth Century*, vol. 1, 191.
55. According to Anne Maclear, there is evidence that many of these cases were settled out of court. *Early New England Towns*, 53; Osgood, *Seventeenth Century*, vol. 1, 191.
56. Channing, *Town and County*, 40.
57. David Thomas Konig, "English Legal Change and the Origins of Local Government in Northern Massachusetts," in *Town and County: Essays on the Structure of Local Government in the American Colonies*, ed. Bruce C. Daniels (Middletown, CT: Wesleyan University Press, 1978), 34; Osgood, *Seventeenth Century*, vol. I, 191.
58. Maclear, *Early New England Towns*, 51.
59. Konig, "Origins," 36.
60. Bridenbaugh, *Wilderness*, 122.
61. Maclear, *Early New England Towns*, 171.
62. Ibid., 159.
63. Osgood, *Seventeenth Century*, vol. 1, 192; Maclear, *Early New England Towns*, 51.
64. C. F. Adams, *Episodes*, 769.
65. Maclear, *Early New England Towns*, 163.
66. Ibid.
67. Ibid.
68. C. F. Adams, *Episodes*, 769.
69. Ibid., 769, 775.
70. R. E. Brown, *Middle-Class Democracy*, 115.
71. C. F. Adams, *Episodes*, 765-766. Latin schools followed the English educational system with a curriculum built around the humanities and the study of Greek and Latin classic languages and works.
72. Bridenbaugh, *Revolt*, 173.
73. C. F. Adams, *Episodes*, 768.
74. R. E. Brown, *Middle-Class Democracy*, 116.

75. See Labaree, *Colonial Massachusetts,* 36, 119. See also Osgood, *Seventeenth Century,* vol. 1, 110.
76. See William Bradford, *History of Plymouth Plantation* (Boston: Little, Brown and Company, 1856), 134-136.
77. Osgood, *Seventeenth Century,* vol. 1, 291, 296-298.
78. Ibid., vol. 3, 233, 337-339.
79. Osgood, *Eighteenth Century,* vol. 3, 207; Francis Newton Thorpe, ed., *The Federal and State Constitutions, Colonial Charters, and Other Organic Laws,* vol. 4 (Washington, D.C.: Government Printing Office, 1909), 2433 ff.
80. Richard L. Bushman, *From Puritan to Yankee* (Cambridge: Harvard University Press, 1969), 35.
81. Bruce C. Daniels, "The Political Structure of Local Government in Colonial Connecticut," in *Town and County: Essays,* ed. Bruce C. Daniels, 54-59.
82. Andrews, *River Towns,* 92.
83. Osgood, *Eighteenth Century,* vol. 3, 277.
84. William F. Willingham, "Deference Democracy and Town Government in Windham, Connecticut, 1755-1786," *William and Mary Quarterly* 30, 3rd Series (1973), 402.
85. Bushman, *Puritan to Yankee,* 3.
86. Andrews, *River Towns,* 78.
87. Bushman, *Puritan to Yankee,* 43.
88. Daniels, "Local Government," 45.
89. Andrews, *River Towns,* 113.
90. Willingham, "Deference Democracy," 407-408.
91. Andrews, *River Towns,* 101-102.
92. Ibid., 42.
93. Bushman, *Puritan to Yankee,* 33.
94. Daniels, "Local Government," 66; Andrews, *River Towns,* 68.
95. Andrews, *River Towns,* 115.
96. Bushman, *Puritan to Yankee,* 54, 63.
97. Andrews, *River Towns,* 75.
98. Bushman, *Puritan to Yankee,* 65.
99. Andrews, *River Towns,* 79.
100. Daniels, "Local Government," 47; Taylor, *Colonial Connecticut,* 45-46.

101. Daniels, "Local Government," 50.
102. Ibid. See also Bushman, *Puritan to Yankee*, 21.
103. Daniels, "Local Government," 50.
104. Ibid., 51.
105. Daniels, *Dissent*, 13.
106. Ibid., 15.
107. Ibid., 98.
108. Ibid., 19, 105.
109. Ibid., 100.
110. Ibid., 96.
111. There were colonial Americans who displayed a marked disrespect for police authority, something with which we in modern America would be familiar. The response one may have received from the town constable for such insolence, however, is something that we in present-day America would be most unfamiliar. Bridenbaugh captures the essence of colonial law enforcement in the following item in the Newport town records: "In 1643, when Job Tyler was summoned to court by the constable, 'he sd he car'd not a fart [or] turd for all their warrants.' Tyler paid for his insolence, however, and was 'adjudged to be whipt till his back be bloody,'" Bridenbaugh, *Wilderness*, 64.
112. Daniels, *Dissent*, 92, 105.
113. Bridenbaugh, *Wilderness*, 163.
114. Ibid., 153.
115. Ibid., 395.
116. Bridenbaugh, *Revolt*, 104, 131; Daniels, *Dissent*, 70.
117. Bruce C. Daniels, *The Fragmentation of New England* (New York: Greenwood Press, 1988), 52; Bridenbaugh, *Revolt*, 173.
118. Bridenbaugh, *Wilderness*, 83; Daniels, *Fragmentation*, 52.
119. Daniels, *Fragmentation*, 49.
120. Bridenbaugh, *Wilderness*, 80.
121. Daniels, *Fragmentation*, 42.
122. Ibid., 47. Daniels further notes that, in some instances, those warned out of town could be put to service at sea.
123. Ibid., 50.
124. Bridenbaugh, *Revolt*, 8; Bridenbaugh, *Wilderness*, 144.

125. Osgood, *Eighteenth Century*, vol. 3, 247-249; Daniels, *Fragmentation*, 50.
126. Daniels, *Fragmentation*, 40, 51.
127. Ibid., 51.
128. Bridenbaugh, *Wilderness*, 157.
129. In fact, Rhode Island used the term councilmen for their chief municipal administrative body.

Chapter Two

THE MIDDLE AND SOUTHERN COLONIES

While settlement in New England was closely regulated, the establishment of new towns in the Middle Colonies—New York, New Jersey, Pennsylvania, and Delaware—was so burdened to a far lesser degree. The practice of using towns as agents of land distribution was not employed in any of the Middle Colonies. Rather, land was purchased by or granted to individuals. On the other hand, one of the Middle Colonies, New York, was first designed as a feudal aristocracy. This plan for New York was eventually abandoned, as settlers avoided the colony altogether or ignored the feudal plan, and formed towns as a direct challenge to colonial authority. These towns were, for the most part, settled by transplanted New Englanders or Dutch settlers.[1]

The early formal structure of New York was centralized—political power rested with a single governing authority. However, a more decentralized system developed in practice. Colonial authority in the rural regions of New York was virtually nonexistent, although New York City was ruled in an autocratic fashion for much of the colonial period. While a county-township structure did exist in

New York, that system was less effective—even chaotic at times—than in New England.

As for New Jersey, a strong system of towns did indeed develop. However, this system developed within an environment that was confused. The status of New Jersey as an independent colony was in doubt for much of the colonial period. Hence, the energy of the New Jersey towns did not have the same effect as in New England.

Private life was strongest in Pennsylvania and Delaware. Religious liberty was arguably at its colonial zenith in these two colonies, in which the county served as the main unit of government. Yet other important local units also existed in these colonies—namely, townships and boroughs. While these systems were hardly even close to the chaotic web of modern American local government, they did not exist within the tight structure that prevailed in New England or even, arguably, New York. Furthermore, like New York City, Philadelphia was ruled as a closed corporation for most of the colonial period. These two cities stand in stark contrast to Boston and Newport.[2]

The less rigorous structure of local government in the Middle Colonies affected both the provision of day-to-day services and the participation of these colonies in wider controversies. The centralized system of Philadelphia proved unwieldy, as the city government failed to even provide basic services. A network of private organizations stepped in to fill the gap. Hardly any recognizable system of public education existed in New York. Services were provided in an uneven fashion as the fiscal system to support these services was regularly in turmoil.

With respect to the participation of local government in issues of wider scope, it may be concluded that they were less effective than in New England. Local units did not have as strong a relative position in their colonies as they did in

Connecticut, Massachusetts, and Rhode Island. This is not to suggest that the residents in the Middle Colonies were indifferent to broader political concerns in America and in Great Britain. For example, a German-born employee of the Dutch East India Company named Jacob Leisler led a successful effort to overthrow the English governor of New York, and controlled the New York colony from 1689 to 1691. The Leisler Revolt (1689) coincides with an uprising in Massachusetts directed against Governor Andros that was supported by several town governments.[3] On the other hand, while Pennsylvania may have been a haven for those seeking a quiet private life, the colony did not provide the kind of leadership exercised by Massachusetts in the crisis leading up to the Revolution. One may surmise that the combination of an unwieldy centralized system and a reactionary loose "polycentrism" makes a local system less able to provide necessary day-to-day services and is less effective in political controversies of a wider scope.

Concerning the settlement of the southern frontier, officials in Virginia and Maryland were keen to establish a system of towns. The residents, many of whom were tobacco farmers, resisted this effort. The formation of towns would make tax collection more efficient, which was something farmers were eager to avoid. The geography of Maryland and Virginia made towns less necessary for commerce than was the case in New England or the Middle Colonies. Navigable rivers traverse the territory that contained these two colonies at regular intervals so that goods could be shipped to ports directly from plantations situated on these rivers.[4]

In the Carolinas one sees a system that was at once centralized and chaotic. The settlement of North Carolina was scattered, as the colony was isolated by swamps and hampered by the lack of a true port for much of the colonial period.[5] This isolation also left the colony at grave risk of attacks from the indigenous population and pirates along the coast. This affected not just the establishment of a local structure but also the development of the colony as a whole. South Carolina was a tale of two settlement patterns. The coastal region was dominated by Charleston, which, in effect, ruled its metropolitan region as a city-state. The local government of Charleston was the de facto government of the colony's coastal region and the government of Charleston was under direct control of the colonial authorities. Greater Charleston was the most centralized of the colonial governments. On the other hand, the interior was largely free from colonial authority and developed a frontier economy based on cattle farming.

The structure of colonial government in the South stands in stark contrast to the system in New England. Local government was generally under the control of colonial authorities. Indeed, in each of the Southern Colonies, and for much of the period before the American Revolution, major local officials were colonial appointees. The system was centralized and inefficient.

No southern colony established a network of towns similar to what developed in New England. In fact, the local government system in the Middle Colonies appears highly developed compared to what existed in the colonial South. For example, the parish system in Virginia had no regular pattern. In theory, a parish is the equivalent of the New England town. However, a parish could be as large as a modern county or as small as a typical New England town. This chaotic structure may have been one of the reasons Thomas Jefferson focused such attention on the reform of local government structure not only in Virginia, but in the whole of the South as well.

As for the provision of local services, the structure of local government in the South affected the Carolinas the most.

Public services in Charleston lagged behind those in cities of similar size in colonial America. In addition, the chaos of North Carolina affected quite negatively the development of that colony. With respect to the participation of residents in issues of a wider scope, the record is more positive.

Several Southern Colonies experienced rebellions, with the most noteworthy erupting in Maryland, Virginia, and North Carolina. The Maryland revolt of 1689 against the Calverts was driven by sectarian concerns.[6] Bacon's Rebellion (1676) in Virginia was a response to the perceived indifference of colonial authorities to Indian attacks on rural settlers.[7] In North Carolina, there was a revolt of a sectarian nature—anti-Quaker (1711)—and another—the Regulator's Revolt (1764)—that was directed against corrupt local officials.[8]

One might argue that the ineffective local structure in the South did not impede the ability of residents to make their opinions heard at higher levels of government. On the other hand, many of these revolts were put down by armed force and did not demonstrate the staying power of those that took place in New England. A pattern that we discerned in our examination of the Middle Colonies can be seen in the Southern Colonies as well. Revolts that are not sustained by a confederation of local units are more likely to be unwieldy and are more likely to be crushed by armed intervention from the home country. Below, we examine the local government structures of the Middle and Southern Colonies in more detail.

New York

System of Local Government

Under Dutch administration, which lasted until 1664, the basic structure of local government consisted of a body of councilmen—called *schepens*—and a *schout*, who took a role similar to that of an English sheriff.[9] The *schepens* also served as a local court, with the *schout* acting as prosecutor.[10] Items under the purview of the *schepens* and *schout* included land issues, fences, roads, and churches.[11] These officers served annual terms, and were selected by the colonial director and council from a list put forward by each town.[12]

The government of New Amsterdam (New York City) consisted of a *schout*, two magistrates (*burgomasters*), and five *schepens*. When the English took control of the region, the so-called Duke's Laws—a comprehensive legal code for the inhabitants of the region, including Indians—were implemented, named after the colony's proprietor, the Duke of York who would shortly become James II. Under the Duke's Laws, the *schout*, *burgomasters*, and *schepens* were replaced by a sheriff, mayor, and alderman, respectively.[13] All of these officers were appointed by the governor.[14] Governor Dongan granted New York City a new charter in 1686.[15] Under "Dongan's Charter," the city was divided into six wards.[16] Each ward would select a constable, assessor, alderman, and assistant. The alderman and assistants of the various wards served on a common council, chaired by the mayor, who continued to be appointed by the governor.[17] The elections in each ward were not, however, fully democratic. Historian Nicholas Varga notes that "these elections were customarily conducted by the incumbent alderman."[18] This system survived until after the Revolution; however, one notable departure from Dongan's system occurred under the Montgomerie Charter of 1731, under which the freemen of each ward were allowed to directly elect aldermen.[19]

The Duke's Laws affected the outlying towns as well. A constable and a body of overseers replaced the *schout* and *schepens*. Under the new provisions, the freemen initially elected eight overseers. Four of the overseers would then be replaced by new officers annually. A constable would be chosen annually as well from among the outgoing overseers.[20] Once in office, the overseers, acting with the constable, would fill other positions, such as surveyor of highways, fence-viewer, and pound-keeper.[21]

Local government in New York was primarily a two-tiered structure after the implementation of Governor Sloughter's 1691 plan of governance, put in place after Jacob Leisler's overthrow and execution. Counties were the primary units, and precincts and townships were secondary. In addition, Albany and New York held special status as cities with quasi-chartered status for most of the colonial period. Prior to 1691, the development of local government grew in fits and starts from an uneven mix of manors, boroughs, towns, precincts, and cities.[22] One reason for the uneven development of towns, especially when compared to that which took place in New England, was the fact that land was granted to individual claimants and not distributed under the authority of the town.[23] According to Patricia Bonomi, colonial administration of the rural areas of New York "was intermittent at best."[24] Despite the reputation of New York as a territory under the feudal boot heel, colonial authorities were mostly indifferent to outlying areas. Bonomi continues: "In the absence of firm central guidelines in the early decades, each community was thrown back upon itself to determine the structure and extent of local authority."[25]

County and Township Government

County government was first installed under Sloughter's reforms in 1691. New York was divided into ten counties, with townships and precincts created as subunits.[26] The 1691 plan called for each county to be governed by a panel of judges and justices of the peace appointed by the governor. In 1703, counties began to be allowed to elect a board of supervisors.[27] Each township or precinct was allowed to send one member to this board, which was responsible for general administration, making ordinances, tax collection, and the appointment of county officers. County judicial authority still remained with justices who were appointed by the governor.[28] Yet even with the remaining authority of the governor to appoint county justices, local freedom had been greatly enhanced. The participatory nature of government in county subunits was reminiscent of that found in New England.[29]

The freemen of each township, gathered in a meeting, selected a board of trustees who would handle the details of local administration.[30] The annual township meeting would also select the township's representative on the county board of supervisors, along with an assessor, constable, fence-viewer, and other officers who oversaw vital town functions.[31]

Education and Social Services

New York colonial government apparently did not consider education a vital function. Unlike the relatively sophisticated system in New England, New York did not provide much public support for schools. Like the elite in Charleston, South Carolina, well-to-do New Yorkers received their education mainly through private tutors, while middle-class families sent their children to church schools of one variety or another. The poor were lucky if they received any education at all. If they did get an education it was likely received as an indentured servant in a wealthier household.[32]

Poverty relief, on the other hand, was a major responsibility of New York towns, as was the case in almost every colonial locale.[33] Municipal relief took the form of direct aid, public housing, and, in later years, almshouses.[34] Churches were primarily responsible for expenses related to relief during the Dutch period, while such responsibilities became more public under the English. But whether the care was private under the Dutch or more public under the English, the towns were keen to avoid these expenses. In 1643, for example, Director Stuyvesant ordered that strangers could not stay in New Amsterdam longer than one night without having their names reported to the town government. Later, in 1684, with New York City under English rule and poor relief becoming more of a regular expense of the secular authorities, constables were required to search the town for strangers and report them to the mayor. Innkeepers were also required to report the names of any travelers who stayed longer than two days.[35] In general, towns were wary of taking on the burdens that legally belonged to other locales. The poor were required to obtain support from their own town and not travel to other municipalities in search of aid.[36] Officials in New York City, like those in Providence, required those receiving public support to wear badges.[37]

Commercial Regulation

Poor relief was not the only closely regulated town activity. Commercial life in a New York town operated under tight supervision as well. For example, in 1648 colonial authorities proscribed non-residents from trading in a town. Boston and Newport had similar regulations, which were primarily aimed at Scottish immigrants who were accused of the ghastly crime of offering goods at cheaper prices than the locals.[38]

The English tradition of the apprenticeship freehold was put into place in New York City. In order to practice a craft or become a merchant, a resident would have to spend seven years as an apprentice and pay a redemption fee. In 1751, the fees were £5 for merchants and 20s for artisans.[39]

A colonial seaport, New York was greatly affected by the trade crisis leading up to the Revolution. The Townshend Acts of 1767, which imposed a tax on commonly used goods imported to the American colonies, precipitated a depression.[40] Local businessmen organized a boycott movement that was, on occasion, enforced by vigilante activity. Mob reaction to the trade restrictions of the Crown escalated in 1770 into a riot remembered as the Battle of Golden Hill, which was followed by the more famous Boston Massacre in Massachusetts.[41]

New York City had its own local cell of the Sons of Liberty and was the scene of significant resistance to British trade policies. Edwin Burrows and Mike Wallace vouch for the patriotic character of the New York colonists, despite the colony's reputation as a breeding ground of royalist sympathies: "Hardcore loyalists were a distinct minority in the province, never amounting to more than 15 percent of the colony's 168,000-odd inhabitants."[42]

Courts

The primary local judicial officers were the sheriff and the justice of the peace. These officers had jurisdiction over civil and criminal matters. In addition, they could oversee administrative procedures in the county.[43] The sheriff had the responsibility to publish proclamations, call and supervise elections, implement court orders, supervise the incarceration of prisoners, and collect quitrents.[44]

After 1691, a regular system of county courts was established. Such courts were authorized to hear cases in which a potential penalty fell short of forfeiture of life or limb.[45] The highest court in the colony was the Court of Assizes, later replaced by a supreme court.[46]

As for the financing of colonial activities, New York relied primarily on revenues from duties on goods moving into and out of the colony, in addition to an excise on liquor. Eighty-five percent of colonial revenues came from these sources. Other funds were derived from quitrents and, if necessary, direct taxation.[47] With the administration of the colony often in turmoil, the collection of taxes in New York was uneven and intermittent.[48]

New Jersey

New York did not recognize the independent status of New Jersey until 1702, when Queen Anne established New Jersey as a royal colony.[49] The ambiguous status before 1702 was largely due to a grant made by James Stuart, Duke of York to John Berkeley and George Cateret, who were recognized as the proprietors of "East Jersey."[50] The *Duke's Release* contained no provisions for Berkeley and Cateret to institute a separate government in New Jersey, but one developed nonetheless.[51]

In the *Concession and Agreement* of 1664, the two proprietors erected the structure of a separate government, and under its provisions the main organ of East Jersey government was a general assembly. The assembly was composed of a body of deputies—representing the various towns—and the governor along with his council, who were appointed by the proprietors. The approval of both the "chambers" was necessary for the enactment of laws. In addition, the proprietors reserved for themselves a veto.[52] Also, a court system was fashioned from the *Concession and Agreement* that would eventually form a three-tiered structure: a local system for minor cases; a county system for large civil cases and felonies; and an appellate supreme court, which also heard capital cases.[53]

The towns were often a source of irritation for the colonial New Jersey government. Town resistance was fiercest over questions of taxation, with the locals resorting to mob violence on occasion.[54] The New Jersey colonial proprietors responded by reasserting their authority in the colony. This retrenchment was detailed in 1676 in the *Declaration of the True Intent and Meaning*, which "clarified" the *Concession and Agreement*.

In fact, the document reads more like a retraction than a clarification.[55] The proprietors reserved for themselves the power to admit residents into the colony, including power over the recognition of land rights. They claimed the power to dissolve the colonial legislative assembly. They further claimed the power to appoint local justices, select church ministers, and solidified the status of the General Assembly as a bicameral body, in which the governor and his appointed councilors would have a separate voice. Government under the *Declaration of Intent* continued until the establishment of New Jersey as a royal colony, although an abortive attempt was made to reform the system through measures in the *Fundamental Constitutions* of 1683.[56]

The government of West Jersey was less complicated and, arguably, more open. This section of New Jersey had a heavy concentration of Quakers.[57] The executive authority resided in a governor and a board of commissioners, selected by the freeholders and proprietors who met as a general assembly. This body also chose other colonial officers and delegated to the towns the authority to select their own officials.[58]

But this dual governing arrangement eventually succumbed to the chaotic situation in the Jerseys. In order to reassert their control within the colony, the proprietors sought the imprimatur of the Crown. In 1702, Queen Anne delivered the *Surrender from the Proprietors of East and West New Jersey* and all of New Jersey was united under a single government.[59]

Pennsylvania

The county was the primary unit of local government in Pennsylvania, with townships as the major subdivisions. Townships in the colony, unlike similar units in New England, did not hold land in common and appeared to have less authority than that which was exercised in other northern locales. In addition to the townships, three boroughs—Bristol, Chester, and Lancaster—had some measure of autonomy with respect to the county. One city, Philadelphia, was ruled by the colonial government as a closed corporation, similar to the arrangement under which New York City was ruled for most of the colonial period.[60]

According to a study conducted by Wayne Bockelman, the responsibilities of county government were wide, and included taxation, courts, poor relief, law enforcement, roads, land management, wildlife management, and vital records. These duties were performed by several officers, some of whom were chosen by the freemen, while the rest were appointed.[61] The elected officials were the commissioners and assessors. Each county had three commissioners and six assessors, all of whom served three-year terms.

In addition, the coroner and the sheriff served annual terms and were appointed by the governor from two nominees provided by the freemen of the county.[62] The remaining county offices, however, were filled solely by appointment.

Each county had several justices of the peace, with each justice having the ability to decide minor cases alone. The justices were appointed by the governor for indefinite terms.

Sitting jointly as a court, the justices could try all cases, except for capital ones, which were reserved for the supreme court. In addition, the justices were responsible for poor relief in the county and for appointing township constables.[63] The following county officers were also appointed by the governor: clerk of the court, recorder of deeds, registrar of wills, and the sealer of weights and measures. The collector of the excise, however, was appointed by the assembly. The county surveyor was appointed by the colonial surveyor-general, the latter being a gubernatorial appointee. Finally, the county treasurer was appointed jointly by the county commissioners and assessors.[64]

Like county positions, those for the township were filled by a mixture of elected and appointed officials. The most important township official was the constable, who assisted the county sheriff. Candidates for this office were nominated by the electors in each township, with the final appointment made by the county justices of the peace in their corporate capacity as a court of quarter sessions.[65] The township assessor along with the inspector of elections were elected by the freemen, while the overseer of the poor and the supervisor of the highways were appointed by the county court of quarter sessions.[66] The boroughs of Bristol, Chester, and Lancaster filled offices in a similar fashion. Unlike the townships, however, boroughs were empowered to make ordinances in a town meeting, making them more like New England towns.[67]

Delaware

Settled first by Dutch and Swedish immigrants, the so-called "Lower Counties"—New Castle, Kent, Sussex—of the Delaware River came under the control of William Penn in 1682. Penn's authority, however, was contested not only by many residents of the Lower Counties but also by the Calverts, who were the proprietors of neighboring Maryland. In the *Charter of Delaware*, offered by Penn in 1701, the Lower Counties were granted permission to form their own assembly.[68] The Lower Counties then formed an assembly in 1704.[69] The Counties, however, retained the governor of Pennsylvania as their chief executive, who had the formal authority to veto legislation.[70] This power, however, was rarely employed.[71] Thus, the assembly was the locus of political authority in the colony. The autonomy of the Lower Counties with respect to Pennsylvania was not finally confirmed until the Revolution, when Delaware declared itself an independent state.

The structure of local government in Delaware was similar to that in Pennsylvania. For example, the town of Wilmington, which received its charter in 1739, was governed in a manner similar to that of a borough in Pennsylvania. The town's electors chose a chief burgess, second burgess, and six assistants, who served collectively as a borough council. In addition, like a Pennsylvania borough, the electors chose a high constable and a town clerk. Furthermore, the borough electors, when gathered in a town meeting, had authority to approve or reject actions taken by the council and to enact ordinances in their own right.[72]

The most important unit of local government in Delaware, however, was the county. The political structure of the Delaware county mirrored that of Pennsylvania. The primary county officials were the justices of the peace, who were appointed by the governor. The justices not only served on the county courts, but they had administrative authority as well.[73] The sheriff and coroner for each county were also selected in a manner similar to that in Pennsylvania. The electors of a county would nominate two candidates each for sheriff and coroner, from which the governor made the appointment.[74] County administration was enhanced by the appointment of officials in smaller units called "hundreds," after the Anglo-Saxon tradition of recognizing a local leader from among one hundred farmsteads. The hundreds, which still exist in modern Delaware, are roughly equivalent to the townships in Pennsylvania and New York.[75] Through an independent assembly and local government structure, the Lower Counties achieved a large measure of independence during the colonial period.

Maryland

While the proprietor held a formal authority that was almost total, Maryland was, in practice, governed primarily at the local level. The strength of the local system was evident in the period when proprietary government was interrupted. Public functions went on, for the most part, unaffected during the unsettled period following the Revolution of 1689, when the Calvert Family—Roman Catholics—were removed from power by the Crown. The most important element of the local polity in Maryland was the county.[76] Most of the political power in a county was held by the county court, whose members had de facto lifetime tenure.[77] Maryland courts had legislative, executive, and judicial authority.[78] The county court consisted of justices of the peace—usually six to eight members—who sat as gubernatorial appointees. However, the governor granted a courtesy to councilors from a particular county, with respect to judicial nominations. The councilors had great influence in the selection of justices in their respective home counties.[79]

To aid the courts in their functions, the governor also appointed a county sheriff and county coroner. The sheriff, an office frequently held by a sitting justice of the peace, not only enforced the law in a county, but also held assembly elections and delivered orders from the colonial government.[80] In addition, the colonial secretary and attorney general appointed two clerks who issued court documents, maintained records, and managed the docket. Furthermore, the county justices selected a variety of officials, as needed, to administer county affairs, the most prominent of which were the constable and highway overseer. The constable assisted the sheriff in maintaining order in the county and also maintained the tax list in each hundred. The overseer of highways, with a court order, could organize residents for labor on the county roads.[81]

The substance of county government included non-felony criminal trials, civil trials, roads, public works, regulating the terms of indentured servants, liquor control, poor relief, weights and measures, and upholding the Sabbath. Colonial courts handled more serious cases. To pay for county activities, the courts had the power to levy a poll tax—a per-head, flat rate that was levied on inhabitants. The poll tax was payable in tobacco, Maryland's cash crop of record. The county levy, however, could be challenged by a county grand jury, from which an appeal could be made to the council and the governor. The assembly curtailed the taxing authority of county courts in 1748. From then on, a county could not set taxes without specific legislation to that effect from the assembly. Thus, the modern practice of placing constitutional or legal limitations on taxation and government expenditure has colonial precedent.[82]

Maryland taxes were low by colonial standards. Most government revenue came in the form of indirect taxes, which, unlike direct taxes in the colony, did not require specific, reauthorizing legislation. Indirect taxes were collected continuously. The primary indirect tax in Maryland was a 2s per hogshead duty on tobacco exports, with half going to support the colonial government and half going directly to the proprietor. Tax policy affected town development, as Maryland lagged behind colonies such as Massachusetts. The establishment of towns would have helped the proprietor in the collection of taxes, and this was something that local governments and the assembly were keen to avoid.[83]

After the Revolution of 1689, the Church of England was established in the colony, and the vestry was added to the body of local governments in Maryland. Originally the governing council of an Anglican parish, membership in the Church of England was not required for a Marylander to serve on a parish vestry.[84] The vestry for each parish kept vital records and could impose fines for moral infractions.[85]

Another unit of local government in Maryland was the special district, which in Maryland was employed in the form of the school district. Other special districts were formed to facilitate poor relief.[86]

Virginia

The territory of Virginia was traversed at regular intervals by navigable rivers. Large tracts of land situated in the hinterlands were not isolated from seaports.[87] Farmers could ship tobacco to markets in England without the need to utilize towns as distribution centers. Unlike Massachusetts, Virginia would not witness the development of a system of towns through which local affairs were managed. The population was more dispersed and isolated.[88] This was in spite of the desire of the colonial government that a system of towns be established. Many settlers that had intended to establish commercial centers in Virginia were thwarted by the remote locations at which settlements were established. As historian Harold Hall describes, the experience of the Huguenot settlers in 1700 is illustrative:

> The Huguenot refugees were greatly disappointed and distressed when they heard of the decision to place them in Manakin Town....They were unprepared for a harsh frontier existence. It must have been obvious that, at Manakin, they would hardly be a community of artisans, craftsmen and merchants. They were not farmers, but they must become farmers out of necessity—learn to farm or die of starvation.[89]

New England local government centered on the town, while in Virginia the county and the parish were the primary local units.[90] Virginia was first divided into eight counties in 1634. By the end of the Revolution Virginia was made up of seventy-two counties.[91] As was the case in Maryland, the county courts were the center of local power in Virginia. A court usually consisted of eight members who served without salary and were appointed by the governor. Hence, the justices tended to come from the elite planter class.[92] In addition to their judicial responsibilities, county justices oversaw a wide range of local affairs, including: highways, bridges, tobacco inspection, construction of mills, tavern regulation, care for orphans, land transactions, ferry regulation—an important function in the riparian colony—and the appointment of officers.[93] Also, the justices set tax rates for the county, the revenues from which were used to pay for services, provide salaries for officers, and provide bounties for predatory animals.[94] The main sources of government revenue were the poll tax and duties on imports and exports.[95]

Virginia county justices also performed the more traditional functions normally associated with courts. The justices heard criminal and civil cases and could inflict punishment and order remedies.[96] County courts, however, could impose capital sentences only for slaves, while other capital trials were heard by the General Court, which consisted of the governor and the councilors.[97] The General Court also served as an appellate court. In addition, appeals could be made to the colonial assembly, although instances of such appeals were rare. As for civil trials, county courts were limited to those involving less than 100 pounds of tobacco, with the crop serving as de facto currency in Virginia.[98] The General Court was the tribunal of original jurisdiction for civil cases above this level.

Figure 2.1: Layers of Government, Colonial Virginia

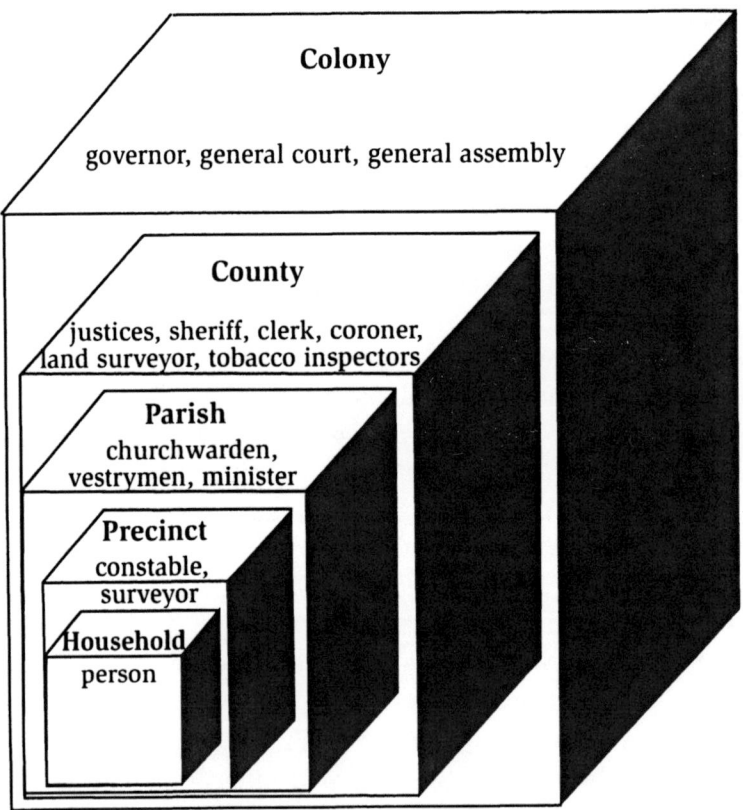

Source: Robert Wheeler, "The County Court in Colonial Virginia," *Town and County: Essays on the Structure of Local Government in the American Colonies*, ed. by Bruce C. Daniels (Middletown, CT: Wesleyan University Press, 1978), 111-113.

The courts were aided in their efforts by a number of local officials. The chief law enforcement official in the county was the sheriff. As in Maryland, the sheriff was appointed by the governor from a list provided by the county justices. The sheriff was typically a justice who temporarily vacated his seat on the court. In practice, the justices rotated the office among themselves. In addition to his responsibilities to keep the peace, the sheriff collected taxes, paid creditors, and supervised elections.[99] The sheriff was assisted by a number of constables who were appointed by the county court. The holding of the office of constable was more widespread among the general population than that of sheriff.[100] Another important county officer was the clerk. This office was filled by gubernatorial appointment. The clerk, however, reported to the colonial secretary and was responsible for court records, vital records, and land certificates. The clerk usually had intimate knowledge of county affairs and the advice of this officer weighed heavily on the court's administration of a colony.[101]

Each county was divided into parishes, along the lines of the model of government in the Anglican Church and, as in Maryland, the parishes were governed by a vestry. This was the limit, however, of the implementation of the Anglican model in Virginia. The colony never had its own episcopal seat.[102] From among the vestry members, a churchwarden was appointed. The churchwarden was the chief officer of the parish. The churchwarden and the vestry enforced religious laws, regulated moral conduct, and were responsible for poor relief. The vestry had the power to levy and collect taxes, the amounts of which could be high, depending upon the needs of a particular parish. The vestry, however, could not try cases of religious inobservance or violation of moral codes. They referred such cases to county courts for adjudication. As slavery became more prominent in the colony, the vestry had the additional responsibility of arresting and selling runaway slaves. Thus, due to the absence of the separation of church and state in colonial Virginia, the effect of the "peculiar institution" (i.e. slavery) manifested itself in a particularly damaging fashion to both civil and religious authority.[103]

North Carolina

Local officials in North Carolina were appointed by the governor until the mid-eighteenth century when the legislature came to possess this power. These institutions, however, remained relatively undeveloped in the colonial period. The highest court in North Carolina consisted of a chief justice and two associates. The chief was appointed jointly by the proprietors while the associate justices were gubernatorial appointees. County courts were able to hear non-capital cases, the justices for which were also gubernatorial appointees. This apparatus was funded by a property tax, the most common source of government revenue in the proprietary colonies of America.[104] And while an Anglican parish system was established, the religious test was discontinued in 1715. The Crown eventually established the royal colony of North Carolina in 1729.[105]

The form of government remained essentially the same in the royal period, with a few changes. The royal governor gained the authority to dissolve the legislature.[106] The court system was augmented by the creation of five superior court districts, in which a justice and assistant could hear cases. Both were appointed by the governor. The colonial seat was moved to New Bern in 1746.[107] The Crown regularized revenues by establishing a 5s per head tax, a tonnage duty, and an import/export duty on liquor.[108] All were standard revenue measures that were employed in other colonies.

South Carolina

Like its sister colony to the north, South Carolina had a frail system of local government. South Carolina did not have an established county court system until 1769.[109] For most of the colonial period, the effective authority in the colony was the municipal apparatus of Greater Charleston.[110] This harbor town was, in effect, a city-state, dependent upon a plantation economy, closely associated with British mercantilism, and ruled by a sclerotic elite.[111] While minor cases could be heard by justices in the hinterlands, the county court of Berkeley—in which Charleston was located—was the de facto civil and criminal venue in the colony.[112] Appeals could be made from the Berkeley court to the governor and council.[113]

The principal local institution in colonial South Carolina was the parish. Between 1706 and 1770, the colonial government created twenty-three parishes.[114] The parish was governed by a board of seven vestrymen, from whom two churchwardens were selected. The vestry was elected annually by the freemen and acted as a parish council. The churchwardens performed executive functions, including the supervision of assembly elections and the enforcement of Sabbath laws.[115] Only members of the Church of England were allowed to serve on the vestry.[116] The vestry was responsible for both civil and religious affairs. They maintained churches, distributed poor relief, built schools, and exercised a limited judicial and law enforcement role.[117] And to aid in the collection of taxes, the colonial government established a board of assessors in each parish in 1703.[118]

The colonial government was financed in a fashion similar to other colonies. Revenues were derived from a mixture of property taxes, poll taxes, duties on liquor and peltry, and a tonnage duty.[119] A specific amount, related to some need, would be set by the colonial government and the requisite property and poll taxes would then be collected. Revenue from duties was episodic, dependent upon the volume of commerce passing through Charleston.[120]

There were, however, settlements in South Carolina that were essentially isolated from the slave plantation aristocracy of Charleston. These settlers established themselves in enclaves as primitive as the early settlements of New England. Their model serves as an alternative to New England in what could be achieved in the rustic conditions of the American frontier.

By the middle of the eighteenth century, the South Carolina backcountry was populated by scores of settlements. These enclaves were located hundreds of miles inland and were settled by squatters. These rural folk paid no quitrents, had no servants or slaves, and did not depend upon commerce with Europe. According to colonial scholar Herbert Osgood: "They were the first genuine frontiersmen who appear in American history."[121] They ruled themselves in an informal fashion, with the cow pen being the focus of civil society.[122] Responding to the desire of these remote settlers to have representation in the assembly, the colonial authorities created two parishes for this region in 1770. This act was vetoed by the Crown.[123]

Georgia

Designed as a haven for the poor and a strategic buffer for South Carolina, Georgia was the last colony to be established by Great Britain.[124] King George II, for whom the colony was named, granted the *Charter of Georgia* in 1732, and it was structured as a non-profit corporation, governed by a Board of Trustees.[125] Until the establishment of royal government in 1752, Georgia was administered more like a municipality than a colony proper. The colonial government was the local government. The members of the board were appointed by the Crown. The board, in turn, appointed a common council. Both the board and council members resided in England.

For the administration of local affairs, the common council appointed bailiffs, recorders, constables, tithingmen, and conservators of the peace. These officers sought advice from the leading board member, James Oglethorpe, as to the administration of affairs. Oglethorpe enjoyed celebrity status in England, through both his military exploits in King William's War and his philanthropic activities. The establishment of the colony was principally due to the force of his personality and his stature within the home country.[126]

Given the unique status of the colony as a charitable endeavor, no board or council member received land grants in Georgia. In addition, land grants were structured to prevent the establishment of large estates.[127] The founders intended the colony to be settled by small-scale farmers, not large-scale planters.

The last colony was intended to be a colony quite different than the first permanent colony, Virginia. It was designed to be the anti-Virginia. Accordingly, slavery was banned, along with strong liquor.[128] In addition, there would be no governor while the proprietors ruled Georgia. Oglethorpe served under the unassuming title of "Treasurer of the Board of Trustees" and left the details of administration to John Percival.[129]

Georgia was a darling of Sir Robert Walpole's Whig administration in Britain. Georgia was the only colony to be directly supported by the Bank of England, which acted as the colony's financial agent. In fact, the Crown continued its direct support even after the proprietorship was disbanded and a royal government installed. About this remarkable state of affairs Herbert Osgood observes, "never before had the British government undertaken the financial support of a colony."[130]

The first decade of the colony's existence witnessed little development and a stagnant economy. The colony was threatened continuously during King George's War (1739-1748). Settlers clung to the few small villages that had managed to form.[131] The settlers begrudged the charitable proprietors for banning slaves that could be used to clear the harsh frontier. In addition, the settlers resented the 500 acre limit on land holdings. Furthermore, the colonists bemoaned the prohibition of strong drink. Accordingly, they smuggled both slaves and rum into the colony, despite the earnest efforts of local constables to prevent such traffic.[132] The proprietors yielded to the colonists, and allowed for the creation of large estates in 1742.[133] This was followed in 1750 by a lifting of the ban on slavery.[134]

In 1751, Georgians were allowed to form their first assembly, the deputies in which represented the towns. The assembly, at first, was limited to offering suggestions. A year later, however, the deputies gained regular legislative authority with the establishment of royal government in Georgia.[135] Thus, the proprietary experiment came to an end.

The legacy of the proprietors, however, lives on in the great achievement that was the creation of Savannah, which remains today as one of the most beautiful cities in North America. Oglethorpe and Percival envisioned a green town, where urban and rural elements would combine through a series of interlocking squares.[136] The town was designed so that there would be alternating town lots, farm lots, and garden lots.[137] Savannah was an Americanized version of the plan that was used to reconstruct London after the Great Fire of 1666.[138]

Conclusion

The less coherent structure of local government in the Middle Colonies affected both the provision of day-to-day services and the participation of these colonies in wider controversies. Services were provided in an uneven fashion as the fiscal system to support these services was regularly in turmoil. The local system in the South also stands in stark contrast to the system in New England. For the most part, local government was under the control of colonial authorities in the South. Major local officials were colonial appointees for much of the period prior to the American Revolution. The system was, on the whole, centralized and, at times, inefficient.

New York, New Jersey, Pennsylvania, and Delaware had a mixed system of county and township government. In addition, there were other municipal units, including the city, borough, and hundred. Tax collection was poorly administered in the middle colonies, with the principal sources being import and export duties, along with quitrents. The principal local unit in New York was the county, which was governed by a board of supervisors. Townships were subunits of the county and were governed by a board of trustees. In addition, the city of New York was governed by a mayor, alderman, sheriff, and other officers. New Jersey had a similar structure to that of New York, although the balance between the county and the township was more equal in New Jersey than in New York. In Pennsylvania, the county was the primary unit and was governed by a board of commissioners. Townships served as the major subdivisions of the county, the residents of which had the power to select local officers. Delaware, which had separated from Pennsylvania in 1704, employed a structure similar to its parent colony, with the notable exception that justices of the peace had a more prominent role.

The Southern Colonies, by and large, had a county system of local government. The principal county officials in Maryland, Virginia, and North Carolina were county judges. In addition to their role as trial justices, these judges exercised considerable administrative authority over day-to-day affairs. The sheriff was the arm of the courts in these counties. Counties were not as well-developed in South Carolina and Georgia. The main subdivisions of southern counties were the parishes; the governing body of a parish was a board known as the vestry. The colonial parish had responsibilities ranging from record keeping, poor relief, inspection of tobacco, to punishing runaway slaves. The parish was particularly strong in South Carolina and, for all intents and purposes, was the main local government unit in the colony. As for Georgia, it stands as a separate case due to its late establishment and the conditions under which it was founded. Georgia was the only colony to receive direct financial support from the Crown. For much of the colonial period, Georgia was run as a municipality.

The more structured systems of New England provided public services in a competent fashion and also fostered activity in controversies beyond the scope normally reserved for local affairs. The less structured systems in the Middle and Southern Colonies also displayed activity in wider affairs, but were much more dependent upon the charisma of a particular individual and, accordingly, had a tendency to fade when faced with an armed response from the Crown or colonial authorities. John Adams and Thomas Jefferson both point us toward a highly structured local system as the best means to provide influence in state and national affairs and the more effective provision of local public services.

✽ ✽ ✽

1. Patricia U. Bonomi, *A Factious People: Politics and Society in Colonial New York* (New York: Columbia University Press, 1971), 5. Bonomi's findings are at odds with those of Carl Becker, *The History of Political Parties in the Province of New York, 1760-1776* (Madison, WI: University of Wisconsin Press, 1909). Bonomi argues that too much is made of the aristocratic nature of colonial government in New York.

2. Bridenbaugh, *Wilderness*, 144; Howard Chudacoff, *The Evolution of American Urban Society* (Englewood Cliffs, NJ: Prentice-Hall, 1975), 5; Judith Diamondstone, "The Government of Eighteenth Century Philadelphia," in *Town and County: Essays*, ed. Bruce C. Daniels 242-244; William O. Winter, *The Urban Polity*, 69; Sam Bass Warner, Jr., *The Private City: Philadelphia in Three Periods of Its Growth* (Philadelphia: University of Pennsylvania Press, 1987), 9.

3. See Michael Kammen, *Colonial New York* (New York: Charles Scribner and Sons, 1975), 122. See also Edwin G. Burrows and Mike Wallace, *Gotham: A History of New York* (New York: Oxford University Press, 1999), 97.

4. Sylvia Doughty Fries, *The Urban Idea in Colonial America* (Philadelphia: Temple University Press, 1977), 111.

5. Osgood, *Eighteenth Century*, vol. 2, 385.

6. Osgood, *Eighteenth Century*, vol. 1, 367; Osgood, *Eighteenth Century*, vol. 2, 204.

7. Louis Rubin offers an apocryphal quote from Charles II concerning Bacon's Rebellion: "That old fool has hanged more men in that naked country than I did for the murder of my father." Louis Rubin, *Virginia* (New York: W.W. Norton and Company, 1977), 24.

8. Osgood, *Seventeenth Century*, vol. 2, 244-246.

9. Osgood, *Seventeenth Century*, vol. 1, 106; Albert E. McKinley, "English and Dutch Towns of New Netherland," *The American Historical Review* 6, no. 1 (1900), 7; Nicholas Varga, "The Development and Structure of Local Government in Colonial New York," in *Town and County: Essays*, ed. Bruce C. Daniels, 188.

10. Varga, "Local Government," 188.

11. Osgood, *Seventeenth Century*, vol. 2, 106.

12. Varga, "Local Government," 189.

13. Bridenbaugh, *Cities in Revolt*, 9.

14. Varga, "Local Government," 192.

15. Varga, "Local Government," 195; Burrows and Wallace, *Gotham*, 92.

Albany received a charter as well in 1686. Bonomi, *Factious People*, 32.
16. The wards were as follows: South, Dock, East, West, North, and Out Ward. Burrows and Wallace, *Gotham*, 92.
17. Selma Cantor Berrol, *The Empire City* (Westport, CT: Praeger, 1997), 12; Burrows and Wallace, *Gotham*, 92. Albany had a similar system.
18. Varga, "Local Government," 195.
19. Bridenbaugh, *Cities in Revolt*, 8.
20. Osgood, *Seventeenth Century*, vol. 2, 122.
21. Varga, "Local Government," 191.
22. Patricia U. Bonomi, "Local Government in Colonial New York: A Base for Republicanism," in *Aspects of Early New York Society and Politics*, eds. Jacob Judd and Irwin H. Polishook (Tarrytown, NY: Sleepy Hollow Restorations, 1974), 33.
23. McKinley, "The English and Dutch Towns," 6, 10.
24. Bonomi, *Factious People*, 29.
25. Ibid.
26. Ibid., 34.
27. Varga, "Local Government," 202.
28. Ibid., 202-203.
29. Bonomi, *Factious People*, 33.
30. In addition to the annual township meeting, subsequent meetings could be called upon petition by three freemen. Ibid., 43.
31. Ibid., 33, 41-43; Bridenbaugh, *Wilderness*, 16.
32. Bridenbaugh, *Wilderness*, 288; *Revolt*, 74; Berrol, *Empire City*, 18.
33. Burrows and Wallace, *Gotham*, 193. In fact, in 1752, as Carl Bridenbaugh notes, the crisis was so severe that churchwardens were forced to borrow £150 in lieu of the following year's taxes. Bridenbaugh, *Revolt*, 122.
34. Burrows and Wallace, *Gotham*, 187.
35. Bridenbaugh, *Wilderness*, 80, 84.
36. Burrows and Wallace, *Gotham*, 145.
37. Bridenbaugh, *Wilderness*, 236; Burrows and Wallace, *Gotham*, 145. According to Burrows and Wallace, the badge had to consist of red or blue cloth with the mark "N:Y" and was sewn onto a person's clothing.

38. Bridenbaugh, *Wilderness*, 45.
39. Seybolt, *The Colonial Citizen of New York City*, 15.
40. Berrol, *Empire City*, 19, 21.
41. The Battle of Golden Hill took place in New York City on January 19, 1770, when American sailor and merchant Isaac Sears and a few colleagues stopped a squadron of British redcoats from posting notices. Several Americans and several redcoats were wounded, and one American killed. See Berrol, *Empire City*, 21.
42. Burrows and Wallace, *Gotham*, 219.
43. Varga, "Local Government," 191.
44. Ibid., 197. Quitrents were taxes directly owed to the proprietor.
45. Ibid., 200.
46. Osgood, *Seventeenth Century*, vol. 2, 116.
47. Ibid., vol. 1, 240.
48. Ibid., 241.
49. Thorpe, *Constitutions*, 2585-2590.
50. Thorpe, 2533-2535. See *The Concession and Agreement of the Lords Proprietors of the Province of New Caesarea, or New Jersey*, 2535-2544. See also Osgood, *Seventeenth Century*, vol. 2, 169, 185-187.
51. John E. Pomfret, *Colonial New Jersey* (New York: Charles Scribner's Sons, 1973), 22. The status of West Jersey was even less clear. See Osgood, *Seventeenth Century*, vol. 2, 171.
52. *Concessions* § I-III, Thorpe, *Constitutions*, 2537-2538. See also Pomfret, *Colonial New Jersey*, 22; Osgood, *Seventeenth Century*, vol. 2, 177-178.
53. Pomfret, *Colonial New Jersey*, 23. See also Osgood, *Seventeenth Century*, vol. 2, 195.
54. Osgood, *Seventeenth Century*, vol. 2, 178.
55. See *Declaration of the True Intent and Meaning of us the Lords Proprietors*, Thorpe, *Constitutions*, 2544-2546.
56. *The Fundamental Constitutions for the Province of East New Jersey in America*, Thorpe, *Constitutions*, 2574-2582.
57. Osgood, *Seventeenth Century*, vol. 2, 252.
58. Ibid., 195-199.
59. *Surrender from the Proprietors of East and West New Jersey, of Their Pretended Right of Government to Her Majesty, 1702*. Thorpe, *Constitutions*, 2585-2590.

60. Wayne L. Bockelman, "Local Government in Colonial Pennsylvania," in *Town and County: Essays,* ed. Bruce C. Daniels, 216. See also Sylvia Doughty Fries, *The Urban Idea,* 88, 95.
61. Bockelman, "Local Government in Colonial Pennsylvania," 216-223.
62. For the origins of this practice see James Wilson, *Works,* vol. 2, ed. Robert Green McCloskey, 550.
63. Bockelman, "Local Government," 221.
64. Ibid., 221-223.
65. Ibid., 223-224. See also James Wilson, "Lectures on the Law: Judicial Department," in *Works,* vol. 2, 461, 469, 472.
66. Bockelman, "Local Government," 224-225.
67. Ibid., 225-227.
68. See the *Charter of Delaware,* 1701. Thorpe, *Constitutions,* 557-561. The provisions for a separate Delaware government would be similar to those for Pennsylvania under the 1701 *Charter of Privileges.* Thorpe, *Constitutions,* 3077-3081.
69. John A. Munroe, *Colonial Delaware* (New York: KTO Press, 1978), 121.
70. Ibid., 124.
71. Ibid., 120.
72. Ibid., 159, 232.
73. Ibid., 231.
74. See Thorpe, *Constitutions,* 559.
75. Munroe, *Delaware,* 218, 232-233.
76. Lois Green Carr, "The Foundation of Social Order: Local Government in Colonial Maryland," in *Town and County: Essays,* ed. Bruce C. Daniels, 73.
77. Ibid., 89.
78. Robert J. Brugger, *Maryland: A Middle Temperament, 1634-1980* (Maryland: Johns Hopkins University Press, 1988), 32, 51; Carr, "Foundation," 73, 74, 86.
79. Carr, "Foundation," 81, 89.
80. Carr, "Foundation," 75; Osgood, *Seventeenth Century,* vol. 2, 71.
81. Carr, "Foundation," 74-76, 85.
82. Ibid., 76, 84-86, 97.

83. Osgood, *Eighteenth Century*, vol. 1, 354-355, 371; Osgood, *Eighteenth Century*, vol. 3, 483-484.
84. Carr, "Foundation," 94. Lois Carr doubts, however, the ecumenical spirit of the vestry: Presbyterians not only voted, but served on vestries for the first ten years or more, and this right was upheld in the 1750s. But despite the wording of the Act, it is unlikely that Roman Catholics or Quakers participated in parish elections. Their attempts to do so would surely have produced protest and an effort to change the law. Quaker records show that, instead, Friends persistently refused to pay parish taxes, suffering consequent attachment of their goods. Possibly some Catholics did the same, although their more vulnerable position probably made such defiance impractical. Carr, "Foundation," 94.
85. Ibid., 93-94.
86. Ibid., 95.
87. Fries, *The Urban Idea*, 111.
88. Channing, *Town and County*, 6; Osgood, *Eighteenth Century*, vol. 1, 350.
89. Harold C. Hall, "Pierre Chastain: Controversy in Manakin Town," (paper presented at the annual meeting of the Pierre Chastain Family Association, Richmond, VA: October 2000), 9. See also Mary A. A. H. Farnsworth-Milligan, *Kith and Kin of the Georgia Ridge* (Newton, KS: United Print., 1973), 25-30.
90. Channing, *Town and County*, 22, 46.
91. Warren M. Billings, John E. Selby and Thad W. Tate, *Colonial Virginia* (New York: KTO Press, 1986), 72; Robert Wheeler, "The County Court in Colonial Virginia," in *Town and County: Essays*, ed. Bruce C. Daniels, 112.
92. Channing, *Town and County*, 51; Wheeler, "County Court," 111, 114. See also Rubin, *Virginia*, 14.
93. Channing, *Town and County*, 45; Osgood, *Seventeenth Century*, vol. 3, 85; Wheeler, "County Court," 115, 120-121.
94. Wheeler, "County Court," 120. As Wheeler notes, however, most civil cases were not complicated. They usually were matters of fact. Wheeler, "County Court," 119.
95. Osgood, *Eighteenth Century*, vol. 1, 337.
96. Virginia replaced this with a jury system in 1643. A head of household was eligible to serve on a jury, which was impaneled by the county sheriff. In an interesting turnabout on the modern

practice, Virginia juries served without food or rest until a verdict was reached. Wheeler, "County Court," 115.

97. Ibid., 118. County courts gained the power to try capital cases involving slaves in 1692.

98. Ibid., 112-113.

99. Wheeler, "County Court," 122. See also Billings et al., *Colonial Virginia*, 72.

100. Wheeler, "County Court," 123.

101. Ibid., 122.

102. William H. Seiler, "The Anglican Church: A Basic Institution of Local Government in Colonial Virginia," in *Town and County: Essays*, ed. Bruce C. Daniels, 135.

103. Channing, *Town and County*, 48-51; Wheeler, "County Court," 113.

104. Osgood, *Seventeenth Century*, vol. 2, 280, 290, 296, 301, 350, 386.

105. William S. Powell, *North Carolina* (New York: W.W. Norton and Co., 1977), 32. See also Osgood, *Eighteenth Century*, vol. 2, 394.

106. Osgood, *Eighteenth Century*, vol. 4, 166.

107. Powell, *North Carolina*, 49.

108. Osgood, *Eighteenth Century*, vol. 2, 400-406.

109. See Richard Waterhouse, "The Responsible Gentry of Colonial South Carolina: A Study in Local Government," in *Town and County: Essays*, ed. Bruce C. Daniels, 161.

110. Walter J. Fraser, *Charleston! Charleston! The History of a Southern City* (Columbia, SC: University of South Carolina Press, 1989), 9; Eugene M. Sirmans, *Colonial South Carolina* (Chapel Hill: University of North Carolina Press, 1966), 250.

111. Walter Edgar, *South Carolina: A History* (Columbia, SC: University of South Carolina Press, 1998), 161. See also Carl Bridenbaugh, *Cities in the Wilderness* and *Cities in Revolt*; and also David A. Smith, "Dependent Urbanization in Colonial America: The Case of Charleston, SC," *Social Forces* 66, no. 1(1987), 1-28.

112. Osgood, *Seventeenth Century*, vol. 2, 279, 300.

113. Ibid., 296.

114. Sirmans, *Colonial South Carolina*, 97; Waterhouse, "Responsible Gentry," 164.

115. Waterhouse, "Responsible Gentry," 165.

116. Ibid., 164.

117. Sirmans, *Colonial South Carolina*, 251; Waterhouse, "Responsible Gentry," 164.

118. Osgood, *Seventeenth Century*, vol. 2, 351.

119. Ibid., 348-350, 360-361.

120. There is evidence that many of these taxes were paid in tobacco. The parish constable was the chief tax collection official in the colony. Osgood, *Seventeenth Century*, vol. 4, 348-349.

121. Osgood, *Eighteenth Century*, vol. 4, 239. See also Louis B. Wright, *South Carolina* (New York: W.W. Norton, 1976), 102.

122. Osgood, *Eighteenth Century*, vol. 4, 241.

123. Allan Nevins, *The American States During and After the Revolution, 1778-1789* (New York: Macmillan Co., 1927), 19-20. See also Robert M. Weir, *Colonial South Carolina* (Millwood, NY: KTO Press, 1983), 276.

124. Fries, *Urban Idea*, 139, 142, 145; Harold H. Martin, *Georgia* (New York: W.W. Norton and Company, 1977) 10, 23; Osgood, *Eighteenth Century*, vol. 3, 35-37.

125. *Charter of Georgia—1732*, in Thorpe, *Constitutions*, vol. 2, 765-777.

126. Osgood, *Eighteenth Century*, vol. 3, 48.

127. Fries, *Urban Idea*, 144-145; Osgood, *Eighteenth Century*, vol. 3, 36.

128. Fries, *Urban Idea*, 148; Osgood, *Eighteenth Century*, vol. 3, 47.

129. Fries, *Urban Idea*, 150; Martin, *Georgia*, 18-19.

130. Osgood, *Eighteenth Century*, vol. 3, 41, 46.

131. Ibid., 54-58.

132. Martin, *Georgia*, 19; Osgood, *Eighteenth Century*, vol. 3, 52.

133. Osgood, *Eighteenth Century*, vol. 3, 57.

134. Ibid, 61-65.

135. Martin, *Georgia*, 31-32.

136. Charles N. Glaab and A. Theodore Brown, *A History of Urban America* (London: The Macmillan Co., 1972), 8. See also Slyvia Fries who first entertains and then dismisses the notion that Savannah was planned this way to suit military needs. Fries, *Urban Idea*, 151.

137. Ibid.

138. Ibid., 156.

Chapter Three

THE FOUNDERS ON LOCAL GOVERNMENT

Despite their well-known disagreements about the shape and character of the American regime, both John Adams and Thomas Jefferson point toward a highly structured local system as the best means for providing influence in state and national affairs and the more effective provision of local public services. Both had high praise for the New England town, and both offered their praise in such a way as to transform our common perception of New England town government.

New England's more structured systems effectively provided public services and also fostered activity in controversies beyond the scope normally reserved for local affairs. By contrast, the less structured systems in the Middle and Southern colonies also displayed activity in wider affairs, but depended more heavily on the charisma of particular individuals. Accordingly, they tended to fade when faced with an armed response from the Crown or colonial authorities.

Local government in the South was more centralized but was, at the same time, weaker. The centralized structure in the South was less efficient and more autocratic, and it will come as no surprise that the more prominent Founders expressed great dissatisfaction with local government officials in the South. In particular, the office of sheriff was a favorite target of their scorn.

The sheriff was appointed by the governor, who in turn was appointed by the Crown. Hence, the local officer that received the greatest opprobrium from the Founders' pens was an appointed local executive that, in the South, operated in a centralized system. Moreover, John Adams and Benjamin Franklin were similarly critical of the office in northern colonies, even though the sheriffs in these colonies operated in a more decentralized context. After our discussion of this appointed executive, we explore the opinions of major Founders on cities and towns, including observations about the New England town.

Sheriffs

The office of county sheriff elicited strongly worded opinions in the writings of the major Founders. The county sheriffs—and deputy sheriffs in particular—were strongly condemned, and were executive appointees, holding office at the pleasure of the governor. Patrick Henry described sheriffs—for which one of the principal duties was tax collection—as "blood-suckers."[1] Nor was his attack simply the partisan rant of an Anti-Federalist. George Washington, John Adams, James Madison, and Thomas Jefferson each recognized the extensive authority wielded by the county sheriff. Jefferson, for example, observed that the sheriff was "the most important of all the executive offices of the county."[2]

The significance of his position derived from the origins of the office: The sheriff was the executive arm of the county court, a role that traces its origins back to early English government. According to Pennsylvania Federalist James Wilson, the formal adoption of the county as a unit of government was made by Alfred the Great (871-899). Sheriffs, however, appear to have been in existence as early as the reign of Egbert (802-839).[3] Wilson describes the English sheriff as an office with "partly judicial and partly ministerial" authority. The sheriff "was the king's servant to execute his writs" and "regulated the courts of justice within the county."[4] In northern states, this role consisted primarily of tax collection and impaneling juries. In the South, however, the roles of the sheriff and his deputies were significantly greater. The courts held a combination of judicial, executive, and legislative authority in southern colonies. As the chief executive of the county court, the southern sheriffs and their array of deputies were even more powerful figures than in the North.

George Washington held these officers in singular contempt. In a letter to his nephew Robert Lewis, penned in 1795, Washington instructed Lewis on how to deal with Virginia sheriffs: "With respect to the Sheriffs, shew them no indulgence; of all descriptions of men in this Country, I think them (tho' there may, and undoubtedly there are many exceptions) the least entitled to favor."[5]

James Madison, while serving in the Virginia House of Delegates, drafted a reform act for the office of sheriff in 1784. Madison appears to have been keen to ensure that sheriffs energetically conducted their appointed functions, but proposed a two-year term limit for under sheriffs.[6] This provision would have limited their time in office and the liability for which they could be held for failing to collect the required taxes. The term limit was eventually removed from the act while the liability protection was retained.[7] The Virginia economy was in a shambles and vigorous tax collection was no doubt harmful to both the collector and the taxpayer. In 1776, Thomas Jefferson proposed that a similar term limit for sheriffs be added to the state constitution, but like Madison's draft reform act, the provision was not included in the final document ratified in June of that year.[8]

The negative opinion of the sheriff's office was not held by Virginians alone. John Adams warned those seeking the office that they might lose their fortunes along with their souls. According to a diary entry by Adams in 1760, many a young man in Massachusetts succumbed to the siren call of the "Deputy Sheriffwick."[9] The position lured office-seekers with the prospect of financial gain. Deputy sheriffs received fees for delivering writs of the court. The position also offered unscrupulous men the opportunity to collect bribes. Such an office could appear tempting to those who saw themselves as trapped in unglamorous occupations: "But shoemaking I suppose was too mean and diminutive an Occupation for Mr. Thomas Hollis, as Wig making was to Mr. Nat Green, or House Building to Mr. Daniel Ward, and he like them in order to rise in the World procured Deputations from the Sheriff."[10] The promise of this office, according to Adams, was seldom delivered. Deputies were held financially responsible for uncollected tax revenue. This fate seems to have befallen the aforementioned deputies.[11]

Writing in January 1776, Adams proposed a model state constitution that made the sheriff an elected position, as opposed to an appointed one.[12] This proposal was drafted by Adams at the request of George Wythe of Virginia. This proposal, according to Adams, was drafted in the form of an anonymous letter that was eventually given to Richard Henry Lee. In June that same year, Thomas Jefferson made his ill-fated proposal to reform the office of sheriff in Virginia. Adams' plan met a similar end in Massachusetts.

The new constitution in 1780, which Adams drafted, maintained the sheriff as an appointed position.

Benjamin Franklin encountered similar corruption in Philadelphia. The constable of the watch was required to round up a number of residents each night to assist him in his duties. Those who declined to assist were required to pay a fine of six shillings. According to Franklin this money "was suppos'd to be for hiring Substitutes; but was in Reality much more than was necessary for that purpose, and made the Constableship a Place of Profit."[13] The constable would then buy some cheap liquor with which to bribe "Ragamuffins" to attend the night watch with him. But the constable and his newly minted "deputies" would routinely fail to perform their responsibilities: "Walking the rounds too was often neglected, and most of the Night spent in Tippling."[14] In 1737, Franklin proposed a plan to fund a regular watch that would be financed by a property tax. Franklin thought the property tax a better instrument of finance than the six shilling fee. This plan, while initially rejected, became the basis for later reforms.[15]

The low regard in which the sheriffs—including deputies and constables—were held by the Founders should not be surprising. Sheriffs were gubernatorial appointees. In turn, the office of governor was a Crown appointee during the formative years of the lives of these Founders. And, going back to its English origins, the sheriff was the arm of the Crown in an English county. Furthermore, the sheriff was the principal tax collector for the county, both in the colonies and in England, and as the King's representative, the sheriff was a readily available target for critics.

However, the Founders—John Adams and Thomas Jefferson in particular—offered further observations about units of government that, at first glance, would be unlikely targets for criticism. One could argue that Jefferson's critique of the city is not surprising, given the overwhelmingly rural character of colonial America. On the other hand, Adams' criticism of the New England town is something about which an account must be made. It is a painless task to cheer on the Founders as they rail against the county sheriff. It is another thing entirely to encounter a Founder expressing skepticism about the New England town, which is one of the most widely admired institutions in the history of American democracy.

Cities and Towns

Thomas Jefferson's critique of the modern city is well-known. The city represented a threat to the health of the individual and to the body politic. His most famous remark with respect to cities is his graphic lament from Query XIX in the *Notes on the State of Virginia*. Unhealthful conditions in cities turn their residents into a corporate affliction, and their festering corrodes the entire nation: "The mobs of great cities add just so much to the support of pure government, as sores do to the strength of the human body."[16] Furthermore Jefferson doubts whether great cities are feasible or desirable: "The yellow fever will discourage the growth of great cities in our nation, and I view great cities as pestilential to the morals, the health and the liberties of man."[17]

At the same time, Jefferson was mindful of the cultural benefits of the city and its ability to nurture the arts.[18] Yet, Jefferson viewed the greater virtue of a pastoral life as worth the sacrifice: "True, they nourish some of the elegant arts, but the useful ones can thrive elsewhere, and less perfection in the others, with more health, virtue and freedom, would be my choice."[19] Accordingly, Jefferson was troubled by the migration of rural residents to the cities. In this, charitable organizations, most notably those devoted to the founding of schools, had been unwittingly complicit in the corruption of rural folk and, hence, of the nation itself: "Even the charities of the nation forgot that misery was their object and spent themselves in founding schools to transfer to science the hardy men of the plough."[20] Such an education, without a focus on practical sciences like agriculture, appeals to the vanity of man and encourages a life of slothful immorality: "The general desire of men to live by their heads rather than their hands, and the strong allurements of great cities to those who have any turn for dissipation, threaten to make them here, as in Europe, the sinks of voluntary misery."[21]

This observation by Jefferson is similar to Adams' criticism of the man who finds shoe-making, wig-making, or house-building ignoble occupations. Such a man then seeks to find a profession whereby he can "live and get Money without Labour or Care."[22] And like Jefferson, Adams observes of such persons that "[m]ost of them decline, in Morals or Estate or both."[23]

The New England Village Revisited

Many people—led by New Urbanist scholars—suppose that the New England town was a compact and quaint village. But the image of the typical New England town as a number of "dwellings and farmsteads gathered purposefully close together and apart from farmlands to form a compact settlement" does not bear the scrutiny of empirical analysis.[24] Joseph Wood, a scholar of colonial geography, observes that:

> The common New England village landscape is burdened by an invented tradition, both popular and scholarly, which has become universalized. In the collective

American mind the New England village is a nucleated agricultural settlement encircling a green and standing for community forbearance in a period of societal discipline and economic stability.[25]

This image was an invention of the Romantics, many of them wealthy urbanites who retreated to such fashionable places as Litchfield, Connecticut, and Concord, Massachusetts, which were among the small handful of center villages that had managed to form by the end of the colonial period.[26] These "summer people" then built upon the model of the center villages as an "architectural retreat" from the increasing industrialism of the city.[27] With the aid of writers like Ralph Waldo Emerson, Henry Thoreau, and Herbert Baxter Adams, this creation of the nineteenth century was read back into the colonial experience, as historian Joseph S. Wood notes:

> Today the settlement ideal, like aesthetic ideology, has become the province of those for whom materialist concerns and preoccupation with symbolic, often historicist, images influence design.[28]

Wood also shows that "Puritan communities were commonly dispersed settlements."[29] The colonial New England landscape was "one of single-family farms and that settlement...resulted largely from an attachment to grassland sites by settlers raising cattle and employing rectangular land division."[30]

William Bradford himself lamented that new settlers to the Plymouth colony "were scattered all over the Bay quickly and the town in which they lived compactly till now was left very thin and in short time almost desolate" and that "no man thought he could live except he had cattle and a great deal of ground to keep them, all striving to increase their stocks."[31] Charles Francis Adams, Jr., in his study of Braintree, Massachusetts, offers a similar observation, "[B]ut those composing this population no longer dwelt together in the neighborhood of Mount Wollaston and about the stone meeting-house. They were scattered over a wide extent of territory."[32]

Thus, Wood concludes that, "The village tradition is invented."[33] The pristine image of colonial towns as a dense collection of stately homes, clapboard churches, and quaint shops surrounding the village green may indeed be so much Romantic mythology. The true colonial New England was a much rougher place than we have been led to believe:

> Colonial New England was a land of modest, dispersed, one-story farmsteads. Nineteenth century elites remade the landscape, which Romantic elites then transformed into an imaginary colonial landscape of stylish houses encircling a town common in a Puritan village.[34]

The town, as a functioning political unit, however, was not invented. The town was real. The town meeting house, where Sabbath services and town meetings were held, was an important place. How, then, do we square this with Wood's empirical analysis?

The New England town, from the colonial period through to the present day, is a political subdivision of the state (or colonial) government. The area of a town may contain rural settlements, urban areas, or mixed concentrations of development. This model was replicated in the form of townships which are important sub-units of government in the states formed out of the Northwest Territory. The colonial New England town was a unit of government that had as its main duties the distribution of land within its jurisdiction, the governing of the residents within the town limits, and the maintenance of a Protestant church.[35] The New England town was not necessarily what we would today call a village. Thus, when we speak of the New England town, we must be careful to remember that, in most cases, we are referring to an agricultural area, dominated by farmers, tending to their flocks in the *town* meadow and working their crops in a private field.

This is not to suggest that the Puritans did not live as a close-knit community. The records indicate that, for the most part, they did live such a life. There was a strong social web in the New England town. The town provided physical security, economic opportunity, moral instruction, and religious formation.[36] The towns of colonial New England were socially, culturally, and religiously homogeneous. The symbol of the town's identity was the meeting house, which was often located in the center of the town. But this center of the New England town was, more than likely, not a center village.[37] Furthermore, this is not to imply that John Adams was an agrarian or that virtue is limited to the rural husbandmen. Strong communities can and do exist in urban areas. Nor is it meant to suggest, as Wood does, that the nineteenth century New England village is in some sense inherently defective. The problem with the nineteenth century New England village was not its structure. It was most certainly handsome in appearance. The problem arises when we read that structure back into the colonial period and then attribute an understanding of local government to the Founders that may have been alien to their own understanding of the phenomenon.

The locales about which Jefferson and Adams made their observations were not altogether different, save for the important fact that the rural polities in New England had a more developed structure than those in Virginia. Jefferson counseled the rural resident to avoid the allure of sophisticated occupations. Adams as well encouraged his fellow rural townsmen to lead an honest life, focused on the mastery of a simple, but useful occupation. On this specific point, at least, Adams and Jefferson concur.

Yet while they agree as to what the good life might be for the average householder, Adams is less sanguine as to the prospects of leading such a good life in the Massachusetts town of the 1760s. Adams describes New England town life as menaced by tavern interests and scheming politicians. After the Revolution, however, Adams changed direction, now finding high praise for the New England town. Henceforth, Adams and Jefferson are of a like mind on the virtues of New England town life. For Jefferson, this praise is consistent with his previous observations of American politics. For Adams it is a reversal from his earlier criticism. Why the change?

The answer to this question provides the key to understanding local government as the American Founders understood that institution. The small New England towns, with all of their defects, initiated an event of world-historical significance. The mustard seed had indeed become a great tree.

John Adams on the New England Town

John Adams detested taverns and their influence on town politics.[38] His earliest comments about taverns appear in a diary entry on May 29, 1760. Adams saw the tavern as a place of entertainment for travelers and a supply depot of liquor for private consumption by town residents rather than an innocuous local pub.[39]

As Adams points out, New England's taverns had become so debauched that they were unfit even for their intended purpose outlined above. We should be careful, however, not to impute to Adams the reputation of a teetotaler. Charles Francis Adams, Jr. offers the following from *Three Episodes of Massachusetts History*:

> To the end of his life a large tankard of hard cider was John Adams' morning draught before breakfast, and in sending directions from Philadelphia to her agent at Quincy, in 1799, Mrs. Adams takes care to mention that "the President hopes you will not omit to have eight or nine barrels of good late-made cider put up in the cellar for his own particular use."[40]

Adams' objection to taverns derived not from any sense that drink itself was sinful or immoral simply, but rather that public taverns corrupted the morals of the youth, destroyed the reputation of a town, and were a bad influence on town politics:

> But the worst effect of all, and which ought to make every Man who has the least sense of his Priviledges tremble, these Houses are become in many Places the Nurseries of our Legislators;—An Artful Man, who has neither sense nor sentiment may by gaining a little sway among the Rabble of a Town, multiply Taverns and Dram Shops and thereby secure the Votes of Taverner and Retailer and of all, and the Multiplication of Taverns will make many who may be induced by Phlip and Rum to Vote for any Man whatever.[41]

In early 1761, Adams wrote that even if a local politician were inclined to reduce the number of taverns, necessity would force such a man to accommodate himself to this commercial interest. A town meeting would likely reject any attempt to reduce the number of public houses. Adams continues:

> The Number of these Houses have been lately so much augmented, and the fortunes of their owners so much increased, that an Artful Man has little else to do, but secure the favour of Taverners, in order to secure the

suffrages of the Rabbles that attend these Houses, which in many Towns within my observation makes a very large, perhaps the largest Number of Voters.[42]

In May of 1761, Adams introduced a motion to be read at a town meeting. After lengthy debate, Adams' measure was approved and restrictions were placed on the number of liquor licenses available in the town. In effect, an official liquor monopoly was created with the intent to limit the spread of taverns. In practice, however, this plan proved a failure.[43]

The consumption of alcohol to excess appears to have been a solvent of Braintree town life. John Adams' great-grandson, Charles Francis Adams, Jr., was of the opinion that this was not a phenomenon isolated in that town. It was a widespread problem throughout Massachusetts and reflective of the general social climate:

> Yet any man of middle life, who has talked of his towns-people and of their families with a Massachusetts man or woman born near the close of the last [eighteenth] century, has been exceptionally placed if he has not heard the same old lamentation. As the name of one after another is recalled, the words, "He drank himself to death" seem so often repeated, that they sound at last not like the exception, but the rule.[44]

Adams had contempt for other elements of New England town life. He was altogether unimpressed with the pompous officiousness of town functions, and the extent to which the town democracy of New England itself could so easily be manipulated by a scheming few. Adams recounts an occasion in which a clique of "Debtors and Labourers" orchestrated a takeover of the Braintree town government. In the midst of a terrible storm, a town meeting was called, and according to Adams, three-quarters of the town was unable to attend. At the meeting, several selectmen were removed from office, including Adams' father. That such a change could occur under such circumstances speaks to all of the bad attributes that have been associated with direct democracy, even in the hallowed towns of New England.[45] These towns were certainly no stranger to "mean and clandestine Artifice, and Plotting."[46] Adams further comments upon the comedy that, according to him, was New England town democracy:

> You may get more by studying Town meeting, and Training Days, than you can by reading Justinian and all his voluminous and heavy Commentators. Mix with the Croud in a Tavern, in the Meeting House or the Training Field, and grow popular by your agreeable assistance in the Tittle tattle of the Hour, never think of the deep hidden Principles of natural, civil, or common Law, for thoughts like these will give you a gloomy Countenance and a stiff Behavior....After attending a Town Meeting, watching the Intrigues, Acts, Passions, Speeches, that pass there, a Retreat to reflect, compare, distinguish will be highly delightful.[47]

Adams, however, did not idly suffer the condition of New England town politics. As mentioned earlier in this chapter, he entered public life through his participation in a special town committee. This committee was devoted to rooting out corruption in the distribution of town common land. Adams would go on to be named the surveyor of highways for Braintree.[48] Although he saw himself as unqualified for the job, Adams set about his task with energy.[49] Adams eventually served as selectman—the equivalent of a city councilman—before entering service on behalf of the colony during the crisis that ensued with the Stamp Act.

A reasonable objection to the above interpretation of Adams' comments could be raised as to his relative immaturity. Adams was a bookish young man who, in his early twenties, felt himself an outsider in Braintree.[50] Hence, his overly critical view of New England town life might be dismissed as so much brooding. As Adams aged, however, his later account of the New England town would be significantly more positive.

But as late as 1814, Adams maintained that his earlier assessment of taverns and the problem they posed was accurate, although his attempts to moderate their influence had proved futile.[51] In addition, the negative comments made by Adams about New England political life were written just prior to the Stamp Act crisis, in which he played a leading role, not only in Braintree but also for the whole colony of Massachusetts. It is, at the very least, plausible that Adams possessed a mature understanding of the nature of New England town life, an understanding that propelled him to do something about it.

More recent scholarship on New England town life corroborates, to a certain extent, Adams' skepticism of colonial local politics. Town residents were reluctant to serve in office. Most of the offices were unpaid and the duties were often viewed as unpleasant.[52] If a person refused to serve in office, a fine would be levied, and these fines were so frequently imposed that they became a regular feature of town finance. In fact, the selection of a town's elite for an office was viewed by historian Robert D. Brown as a form of taxation—of time and effort—on the wealthier residents of a town.[53]

As for the frequency of town meetings, they were called more often during the first few years of a town's existence. Anne Bush Maclear found that for the Massachusetts towns of Cambridge and Dorchester, town meetings were typically held once a month in the formative years with the frequency declining to two or three per year as the town matured.⁵⁴ This pattern turns out to have been common for New England town meetings in general.⁵⁵ During periods of controversy, however, such as occurred during the Stamp Act crisis, meeting frequency increased. Furthermore, despite the infrequency of town meetings, poor attendance was a common problem. The practice of imposing fines for failing to attend meetings indicates that poor attendance was a problem. And such fines were commonly levied. Low attendance was the norm. Evidence from Rhode Island suggests that even highly attended meetings did not exceed 30 percent of the adult males.⁵⁶ This pattern appears to have been repeated in Connecticut and Massachusetts as well.⁵⁷ The young Adams' account of the removal of three selectmen by a small clique of intriguers at a sparsely attended meeting appears to be closer to the rule than the exception. Thus, Adams' own understanding of New England political life is somewhat at odds with Tocqueville's now legendary assessment of New England town life.

Tocqueville did praise the New England town for its independent position within the political structure of American government. In this, there is nothing to distinguish him from Adams or any other Founder for that matter; perhaps even Madison. Where Adams' self-understanding of New England local politics seemed to depart from Tocqueville's observations lie in the latter's appellation of the New England town as a nursery of the virtuous democratic soul.

Consider Tocqueville's comment that, "The institutions of a township are to freedom what primary schools are to science; they put it within reach of the people; they make them taste its peaceful employ and habituate them to making use of it."⁵⁸ Consider further Tocqueville's description of the unproblematic love a town member can devote to his locale:

> The New England township is so constituted that it can serve as the home of lively affections, and at the same

time nothing is next to it that strongly attracts the ambitious passions of the human heart...these passions, which so often trouble society, change character when they can be expressed so near the domestic hearth and in a way in the bosom of the family.[59]

The New England township, in Tocqueville's rosy account, is a place where "the storms of municipal life are few."[60] Adams and the Founders have expressed a less idealized view.

This is not to suggest that Tocqueville's analysis was somehow superficial. There can be no question that Tocqueville's overall analysis in *Democracy in America* is nuanced, nor should we read Tocqueville so that we can clip from the great manuscript snippets that suit our individual arguments. However, the common understanding of the New England town has been influenced by the few snippets above. Certainly, for our purposes, Tocqueville's specific comments above are not consistent with the view of the New England town as Adams understood it. Adams came to respect the New England town in spite of itself.

Subsequent scholarship suggests that our understanding of the New England town needs correction. The misunderstanding is, in part, the result of a lack of information. Such information can be had from the studies of colonial scholars. On the other hand, some of the misunderstanding results from our inability to face some unpleasant facts. The New England towns were independent and "democratic" due largely to the homogeneity of the population, in social, economic, and religious terms. This homogeneity, in turn, was due in large measure to strict and sometimes harsh policies including the exclusion of the poor from town membership at the pain of corporal punishment, denial of land ownership without proper character references, banishment for heresy, and capital punishment for heresy.

One may attempt to explain away such policies in light of the political and religious context of the Reformation struggle in England and, paraphrasing the Declaration of Independence, the conditions that required large groups of people to seek refuge in America. All of this can, as a matter of argument, be granted. What is more difficult to grant, however, without seriously compromising the argument, is the Romantic perceptions of the New England polity as one that should be admired for its superior civic spirituality. Tocqueville appears to be aware of this, praising the structure of local government in New England, in addition to its spiritual qualities.[61] These comments, however, are not as much a part of New England town lore as those extolling the emotional purity of New England town membership.

New England town democracy was in many ways a brutal institution. As mentioned above, Madison's analysis of factions in *The Federalist* 10 may be applied directly to the New England town:

> From this view of the subject it may be concluded that a pure democracy, by which I mean a society consisting of a small number of citizens, who assemble and administer the government in person, can admit of no cure for the mischiefs of faction. A common passion or interest will, in almost every case, be felt by a majority of the whole; a communication and concert results from the form of government itself; and there is nothing to check the inducements to sacrifice the weaker party or an obnoxious individual. Hence it is that such democracies have ever been found incompatible with personal security or the rights of property; and have in general been as short in their lives as they have been violent in their deaths. Theoretic politicians, who have patronized this species of government, have erroneously supposed that by reducing mankind to a perfect equality in their political rights, they would at the same time be perfectly equalized and

assimilated in their possessions, their opinions, and their passions.[62]

Furthermore, consider once again the following from Madison: "A religious sect may degenerate into a political faction in a part of the Confederacy; but the variety of sects dispersed over the entire face of it must secure the national councils against any danger from that source."[63]

Little in John Adams' accounts of colonial local politics—not to mention the results of recent scholarship—would prevent us from applying Madison's analysis to New England local politics. Yet, by the time Madison had formed these opinions, not only Jefferson, but Adams as well, extolled the virtues of the New England town. This evaluation of the town—and for Adams it was a reevaluation—was not conducted blindly. Neither Adams nor Jefferson understood the primary importance of the New England town as an entity that embodied some notion of local spiritualism. Jefferson's admiration of the New England towns came partly as a result of their successful efforts to undermine the Embargo Act passed late in his second term as President. Both Adams and Jefferson respected the New England town as the cradle of the American Revolution. For Jefferson, the virtues of town life would not be in the service of a civic spiritualism, at least not one understood apart from maintaining the Revolution that had affected the entire nation. For these two Founders, the New England towns were not admired so much for what they *were*, but instead for what they *did*; not for their spirit but for their deeds. And they were admired not just for any deed, such as the proper building of a road or any other such public works project.

The towns were admired by these two great men for their role as institutions of a political character, understood in the most fundamental sense. As the most primitive level of government, local institutions bear an unusual—albeit rare—responsibility as the last rampart amidst the state of nature. With their brutal heritage, sometimes corrupt politics, and questionable social climate, the New England towns passed the ultimate test of any polity: perseverance in the extreme political moment. The defining image of the New England townsman—if Adams and Jefferson are to be believed—is not that of a contented burgher, happily deliberating in the meeting house as to the proper route for the latest cart path, with said burgher then returning home to happily regale his family with the spiritual glories of civic participation.

For better or worse, the defining image of the New England townsman is that of a crusty tavern dweller, abruptly ending his idle conversations, casting aside his tobacco pipe, grabbing his musket, facing the King's troops on the town green, and thereby risking death or mutilation—perhaps with rum on his breath. The protection of the rights to life, liberty, and the pursuit of happiness is both a *decent* and *practical* endeavor. It is in this light that Adams and Jefferson understood the theoretical implications of local government and the American Founding.[64]

Praise for the New England Town

When Adams changed his opinion of the New England town he was under no illusion about the dangers of taverns, political corruption, and peculiar factions within the town and the harmful effect each could have on civic life. His opinions in this regard did not change.[65]

The performance of the towns, however, from the onset of the Stamp Act crisis through to the Revolution itself transformed, in Adams' mind, the towns, in spite of their other faults. Adams takes the radical step of reassessing all of the faults he found in the towns—faults that were real—and reading their successful stand against the Crown back into the character of the towns themselves. The towns, by their heroic stand against the Crown, had sanctified themselves, beyond our mere powers to add or detract:

> Major Langbourne dined with us again [on July 21, 1786]. He was lamenting the difference of character between Virginia and New England. I offered to give him a receipt for making a New England in Virginia. He desired it; and I recommended to him town meetings, training days, town schools, and ministers, giving him a short explanation of each article. The meeting-house and school-house and training field are the scenes where New England men were formed. . . . In all countries and in all companies, for several years, I have in conversation and in writing, enumerated the towns, militia, schools, and churches, as the four causes of the growth and defence of New England. The virtues and talents of the people are there formed; their *temperance*, patience, fortitude, prudence, and justice, as well as their sagacity, knowledge, judgment, taste, skill, ingenuity, dexterity, and industry.[66]

Adams' attribution of temperance to the character of New England townsmen is stunning; it speaks volumes as to the light in which he understood local government and town life. Once the blood of the Revolution had been shed, he could not look at the towns in the same way. More incredibly, Adams' understanding of the tavern itself changed. According to Charles Francis Adams, Jr. his great-grandfather bore witness to the potency of the tavern as a "political educator and influence."[67] Consider Adams' discussion of the tavern as political educator below, from which I quote at length:

> Within the course of the year before the meeting of Congress, in 1774, on a journey to some of our circuit courts in Massachusetts, I stopped one night at a tavern

> in Shrewsbury, about forty miles from Boston, and as I was cold and wet, I sat down at a good fire in the barroom to dry my greatcoat and saddlebags till a fire could be made in my chamber. There presently came in, one after another, half a dozen, or half a score, substantial yeoman of the neighborhood, who, sitting down to the fire after lighting their pipes, began a lively conversation upon politics. As I believed I was unknown to all of them, I sat in total silence to hear them. One said, 'The people of Boston are distracted.' Another answered, 'No wonder the people of Boston are distracted. Oppression will make wise men mad.' A third said, 'What would you say if a fellow should come to your house and tell you he was come to take a list of your cattle, that Parliament might tax you for them at so much a head? And how should you feel if he was to go and break open your barn, to take down your oxen, cows, horses and sheep?' 'What should I say?' replied the first; 'I would knock him in the head.' 'Well,' said a fourth, 'If Parliament can take away Mr. Hancock's wharf and Mr. Rowe's wharf, they can take away your barn and my house.' After much more reasoning in this style, a fifth, who had as yet been silent, broke out, 'Well, it is high time for us to rebel now than at any time to come. If we put it off for ten or twenty years, and let them go on as they have begun, they will get a strong party among us, and plague us a great deal more than they can now. As yet, they have but a small party on their side.'...I mention this anecdote to show that the idea of independence was familiar even among the common people much earlier than some persons pretend.[68]

The admission that "the idea of independence was familiar even among the common people, much earlier than some persons pretend" is an important one. Perhaps one of those "persons" was Adams himself. Perhaps his assessment of New Englanders had been all wrong.

Adams did not condone the carousing that takes place in the tavern. He did not sit down with them and smoke tobacco and drink "Phlip." He did not join the dialogue.

He simply sat there as the stranger, letting the interlocutors speak for themselves. There can be no question that Adams would have preferred those hearty yeoman to have gathered somewhere other than in a local tavern, but gather in the local tavern they did.

As noted above, this reevaluation of New England townsmen began to take shape during the Stamp Act crisis. Below, Adams makes the incredible statement that before the Stamp Act, men were judged on their individual merits. After the Stamp Act, all that seemed to matter was their opinion on the Stamp Act. The Act has transformed the people of New England:

> Such and so universal has been the Resentment of the People, that every Man who has dared to speak in favour of the Stamps, or to soften the detestation in which they are held, how great soever his Abilities and Virtues had been esteemed before, or whatever his fortune, Connections and Influence had been, has been seen to sink into universal Contempt and Ignominy. The People, even to the lowest Ranks, have become more attentive to their liberties, more inquisitive about them, and more determined to defend them, than they were ever before known or had occasion to be. Innumerable have been the Monuments of Wit, Humour, Sense, Learning, Spirit, Patriotism, and Heroism, erected in the several Colonies and Provinces, in the Course of this Year. Our Presses have groaned, our Pulpits have thundered, our Legislatures have resolved, our Towns have voted, The Crown Officers have every where trembled, and all their little Tools and Creatures, been afraid to Speak and ashamed to be seen.[69]

Later, in his 1787 *Defence of the Constitutions of Government of the United States of America*, Adams interprets the whole history of American colonial government as leading to the moment of rebellion. Consider again a passage from Adams' letter to Abbé de Mably, referenced in a footnote in our Chapter One above. Adams makes the case that:

> There is a general analogy in the governments and characters of all the thirteen states; but it was not till the debates and the war began in Massachusetts Bay, the principal province of New England, that their primitive institutions produced their first effect.[70]

This is a remarkable statement by Adams. Essentially, the institutions did not amount to much until they showed their mettle in the struggle with England. This is particularly striking since, as we know, the government of the colonies was, for the most part, local government. These local governments, in particular the New England towns, did not come to *be*, in a fundamental sense, until their struggle with England. In a subsequent passage from the same letter, from which I quote at length, Adams continues upon the same theme, with the "subject" being the American Revolution:

> Four of these institutions ought to be amply investigated and maturely considered by any person who wishes to write with correct information upon this subject....The four institutions intended are: 1. The towns or districts[;] 2. The congregations[;] 3. The schools[;] 4. The militia. The towns are certain extents of country, or districts of territory into which Massachusetts Bay, Connecticut, New Hampshire, and Rhode Island, are divided. These towns contain upon average, say six miles or two leagues square. The inhabitants who live within these limits are formed by law into corporations, or bodies politic, and are invested with certain powers and privileges, as, for example to repair the great roads or highways, to support the poor, to choose their selectmen, constables, collectors of taxes, and above all, their representatives in the legislature; as also, the right to assemble, whenever they are summoned by their selectmen, in their town halls,

there to deliberate upon the public affairs of the town, or to give instructions to their representatives in the legislature. The consequences of these institutions have been, that the inhabitants, having acquired from their infancy the habit of discussing, of deliberating, and of judging public affairs, it was in these assemblies of towns or districts that the sentiments of the people were formed in the first place, and their resolutions were taken from the beginning to the end of the disputes and the war with Great Britain.[71]

Adams portrays the entire history of the New England towns—with all of their necessary day-to-day functions—as a preparation for their great confrontation with England. This is what made them special places. They were not special for the deliberation upon and conduct of affairs, understood, in their own right, as civic spiritualism.

Adams thought the key characteristic that aided them in this effort was the fact that each town, as a town, was represented in the colonial legislature. The loss of this feature in modern local government has no doubt contributed to its decline in power vis-à-vis state and national governments. The Anti-Federalists concurred with Adams in this regard. And remarkably, as far as state legislatures were concerned, Madison concurs as well.

It was the shared position of a broad sweep of political views in the Founding period, that recognizable local units, be they counties in the South or towns in the North, should be the basis of representation in the state legislature, as they had been for colonial legislatures. And the motivation was not some geographical fussiness. The reasons lie in the proper representation of particular interests. District lines drawn without regard to local conditions will lead to a disconnection between the electors and the elected. It would be difficult to dispute Patrick Henry's near prescient analysis of what would happen to congressional districts when drawn without regard for local political boundaries:

> If your elections be by districts instead of counties, the people will not be acquainted with the candidates. They must therefore be directed in the elections by those who know them. So that instead of a confidential connection between the electors and the elected, they will be absolutely unacquainted with each other. A common man must ask a man of influence how he is to proceed, and for whom he must vote. The elected, therefore, will be careless of the interest of the electors. It will be a common job to extort the suffrages of the common people for the most influential characters. *The same men may be repeatedly elected by these means. This, Sir, instead of promoting the freedom of elections, leads us to an Aristocracy.*[72]

In a letter to John Brown of Kentucky, written on August 23, 1785, James Madison concurs with the argument made by Patrick Henry, as far as state legislatures were concerned. Below, Madison discusses the method by which representatives would be chosen for the Kentucky legislature. Since Kentucky derived its heritage of local government from the southern tradition, the primary local unit was the county. In the letter, Madison adheres to a system of representation that would focus on weighing each region by population. There are two primary ways to accomplish this. First, draw county boundaries so that each has an equal population. The second method would be to leave intact the present county boundaries and weight the number of electors per county according to population. Madison considers the rewriting of county boundaries impractical and favors the proportional method:

> By the plan of representation I mean: 1. The classing of the electors. 2. The proportioning of the representatives to each class. The first cannot otherwise be done than by geographical description, as by Counties. The second

may easily be done, in the first instance, either by comprising within each County an equal number of Electors, or by proportioning the number of representatives of each County to its number of Electors. The difficulty arises from the disproportionate increase of electors in different Counties. There seem to be two methods only by which the representation can be equalized from time to time. The first is to change the bounds of the Counties; the second, to change the number of representatives allotted to them, respectively. As the former would not only be most troublesome and expensive, but would involve a variety of other adjustments [local officers, etc.], the latter method is evidently the best.[73]

Madison advocates a system for local representation in the state legislatures that comports with Patrick Henry's plan and certainly with what Adams said was the most important factor in establishing the local units of New England as the cradles of the Revolution, a revolution that, according to Adams, would change the course of human history. When confronted in 1780 with the claim that Americans, after a while, would return to the bosom of the British Empire, Adams responded that the towns, among others would not allow it, even if this plan were designed by those in loftier positions:

> To say that the Americans are upon the poise, are balancing, and will return to their allegiance to the King of England, is as wild as bedlam...Ask the town meetings,— those assemblies which dared, readily enough, to think as they pleased, and say what they would, dared attack the king, lords, commons, governors, council, representatives, judges, and whole armies, under the old government, and which attack everybody and every thing that displeases them at this day!...The Americans at this day have higher notions of themselves than ever. They think they have gone through the greatest revolution that ever took place among men; that this revolution is as much

for the benefit of the generality of mankind in Europe as for their own.[74]

Thus, the corrupt little burghs, beset by rum and rapacious hacks, came to shake the political world to its foundation. Adams mentions these towns again in light of their position in the regime, not in terms of the functions they perform as local entities, nor as mystical incubators of the local civic soul. Also note that Adams thinks that the Americans have a higher opinion of themselves than they ever had before.

Finally, Adams extends the true spirit of the New England town into the American regime after its independence. In his most radical statement regarding the towns, Adams contends that they would be there to remind those office holders in the new republic that the Revolution continues. Note the universal application of this sentiment to the people, in the statement regarding the worth of each person, "high or low":

> The press, the towns, the juries, and the assemblies are four sources, from whence an unerring demonstration of the true sentiments of the people of America may be drawn....The towns in many parts of America are small districts of territory, on an average perhaps six miles square. By the ancient laws of the country, which are still in force, any seven inhabitants of one of these towns have a right to demand of the magistrates a public assembly of all. There are necessarily several of these town meetings every year, and generally a great number of them. In these assemblies, every man, high and low, every yeoman, tradesman, and even day-laborer, as well as every gentleman and public magistrate, has a right to vote, and to speak his sentiments upon public affairs, to propose measures, to instruct the representatives in the legislature, &c. This right was constantly and frequently used under the former government, wherein they enjoined an open opposition to judges, governors, acts of parliament, king,

lords, and commons of Great Britain. What is there now to prevent them from opposing Congress? Nothing.⁷⁵

It is only a small step from the thoughts expressed by John Adams about the New England town to those expressed by Thomas Jefferson in his famous ward republic proposal, which Hannah Arendt claims was Jefferson's most cherished political idea.⁷⁶ Adams and Jefferson shared a radical understanding of local government and the American Founding. Geographically identifiable political units, understood as such, stand as the last line of defense against centralized tyranny, foreign or domestic. And this resistance could occur in spite of the routine and petty corruption that comes with local administration. While there can be no doubt that corruption, petty or otherwise, is a solvent of civil society, the greater corruption comes from the failure to recognize the higher purpose of local government, as Adams and Jefferson understood that purpose.

Jefferson's Ward Republics

Jefferson considered the creation of ward republics as one of the two most important elements on which the future of the national republic depended. The other was the creation of a public education system. In a Letter to Governor John Tyler in 1810, Jefferson mentions his plan, referring to wards by their ancient name, "hundreds":

> I have indeed two great measures at heart, without which no republic can maintain itself in strength. 1. That of general education, to enable every man to judge for himself what will secure or endanger his freedom. 2. To divide every county into hundreds, of such size that all the children of each will be within reach of a central school in it.⁷⁷

Jefferson's ward proposal was mentioned again in a letter to John Adams in 1813. Note that Jefferson used language almost identical to Adams' description of the New England town. In Adams' letter to Congress in 1780, he described a town as follows: "The towns in many parts of America are small districts of territory, on an average perhaps six miles square."[78] Jefferson puts forth his version of what the New England town would be when transplanted to Virginia:

> This [bill] proposed to divide every county into wards of five or six miles square, like your townships; to establish in each ward a free school for reading, writing and common arithmetic; to provide for the annual selection of the best subjects from these schools, who might receive, at the public expense, a higher degree of education at a district school; and from these district schools to select a certain number of the most promising subjects, to be completed at an [sic] university, where all the useful sciences should be taught.[79]

And in an 1824 letter to Major John Cartwright, Jefferson again clearly establishes the model for his ward republics on Adams' description: "I hope [Virginia] will adopt the subdivision of our counties into wards. The former may be estimated at an average of twenty-four miles square; the latter should be about six miles square each."[80]

Beyond their function as elements of a statewide education system, the ward would be a regular element of local government, providing local services. The wards would combine to make a county, the counties would form the state, and the states would form the Union.[81] These wards would have responsibilities similar to that of the New England township.[82] In a letter to John Adams, Jefferson further describes the regular municipal functions that the wards would fulfill:

> My proposition had, for a further object, to impart to these wards those portions of self-government for which they are best qualified, by confiding to them the care of their poor, their roads, police, elections, the nomination of jurors, administration of justice in small cases, elementary exercises of militia; in short, to have made them little republics, with a warden at the head of each, for all those concerns which, being under the eye, they would better manage than the larger republics of the county or State.[83]

But there was more to Jefferson's ward republic plan than a properly ordered administration of local affairs. According to Hannah Arendt, Jefferson's ward system, "with an almost weird precision," anticipated the *soviets* and *Räte* that made their appearance in "every genuine revolution" in the nineteenth and twentieth centuries.[84] These councils or local organizations were at odds with what might be labeled as the centralizing tendencies of the leaders of these revolutions. The leaders, according to Arendt, "[F]ailed to understand to what extent the council system confronted them with an entirely new form of government, a new public space for freedom which was constituted and organized during the course of the revolution itself."[85] The wards would, according to Jefferson, help maintain the true spirit of the Revolution and offset the potentially ossifying tendencies of national regimes:

> I have long contemplated a division of [Virginia] into hundreds or wards, as the most fundamental measure for securing good government, and for instilling the principles and exercise of self-government into every fibre of every member of our commonwealth.[86]

Going one step further, Jefferson envisions the republic, as produced in miniature, in the rule of a man over his own farmstead. Thus, the republic is projected out from the household, to the ward, to the county, to the state, and then onto the national level, invigorating all.[87]

Arendt believed that Jefferson saw the ward system as the "[o]nly possible non-violent alternative to his earlier notions about the desirability of recurring revolutions."[88] The ward system would institutionalize the revolution. It simultaneously would check the tyrannical tendencies of the central government and the enervating tendencies of a private local life. In a letter to Samuel Kercheval, written July 12, 1816, Jefferson makes this clear; his comment below occurs in the midst of one of his most radical statements about democracy in America. Democracy, he wrote, was for the living, not the dead. And our adherence to old forms should be held as long as these prove useful to the continuance of the republic. If not, then innovation is allowed. And such innovation, were it to be peaceful, would best be made through the workings of the ward system. Questions of great importance could be directly considered by ward members. While the immediate question concerning Jefferson in this letter revolved around national finance, one could imagine any major issue coming before a ward meeting in such a fashion:

> Here, then, would be one of the advantages of the ward division I have proposed. The mayor of every ward, on a question like the present, would call his ward together, take the simple yea or nay of its members, convey these to the county court, who would hand on those of all its wards to the proper general authority; and the voice of the whole people would be thus fairly, fully, and peaceably expressed, discussed, and decided by the common reason of society. If this avenue be shut to the call of sufferance; it will make itself heard through that of force, and we shall go on, as other nations are doing, in the endless circle of oppression, rebellion, reformation; and oppression, rebellion, reformation, again; and so on forever.[89]

Jefferson had direct knowledge of the power of local units of government, when properly organized, to affect *national* affairs. This was not only true of the Revolution itself, but also during the controversy over Jefferson's Embargo Act. In this crisis, the New England towns were able, as Adams had predicted in 1780, to defy a national government. And not only did they defy the national government, but, according to Jefferson, the New England towns defied the will of the national majority:

> How powerfully did we feel the energy of this organization in the case of the embargo? I felt the foundations of the government shaken under my feet by the New England townships. There was not an individual in their States whose body was not thrown with all its momentum into action; and although the whole of the other States were known to be in favor of the measure, yet the organization of this selfish little minority enabled it to overrule the Union. What would the unwieldy counties of the Middle, the South, and the West do? Call a county meeting, and the drunken loungers at and about the court-houses would have collected, the distances being too great for the good people and the industrious generally to attend. The character of those who really met would have been the measure of the weight they would have had in the scale of public opinion. As Cato, then, concluded every speech with the words, 'Carthago delenda est,' so do I every opinion, with the injunction, 'divide the counties into wards.'[90]

Jefferson laments the lack of townships in the south, middle, and west of the United States. Had these regions been organized according to wards, things might have been different in the Embargo Act controversy. While his admiration is grudging for this "selfish little minority," it is admiration nonetheless. One can detect an echo from Adams in Jefferson's description of those who failed to resist the "selfish minority." Jefferson describes them as "drunken loungers," as Adams had described the New England townsmen before the Revolution. For Adams, his "drunken loungers" in the New England town had redeemed themselves through the blood of the Revolution. But one is left to ponder whether or not a "drunken lounger" in Jefferson's America could ever redeem himself. With this statement having been made about events in 1807, one wonders, at the time, how many of these "drunken loungers" were veterans of the War of Independence? In Jefferson's America, the Revolution continues and it cannot be said to have been achieved at any particular point. It is almost as if Jefferson has subscribed to a doctrine of political Calvinism, in that one never truly knows whether or not one is "elected" (i.e., saved). In this respect, Jefferson may have held more steadfastly to the Puritan heritage than did his great friend and rival from New England.

The martial quality of wards lies not far below the surface. The wards would be to national political crises as militia are to foreign or domestic military threats. The workings of the wards, as described by Jefferson below, are reminiscent of the Greek phalanx.[91] Jefferson's yeoman farmer could, in a question of political controversy, move rather quickly from his private affairs to the field of battle, with very little warning. Due to the simple yet powerful organization of the wards, the yeoman farmer would require very little in political drill or training in order to have a devastating impact in a crisis.[92]

Jean Yarbrough concurs with Arendt that, indeed, wards were at the "heart of his mature understanding of republicanism," an understanding that went beyond the mere maintenance of institutional forms.[93] Without the proper revolutionary character, even the most cleverly constructed republic might not last.[94] Understood in such a way, ward republics reveal the radical character of Jefferson's politics, the politics of perpetual revolution.⁹⁵ Michael Zuckert also acknowledges that ward republics were "the most remarkable and probably the most important feature of Jefferson's system."⁹⁶ Zuckert adds that Jefferson "had a point of continuing value, and that the amalgam for which he stands continues to have power in the political culture."⁹⁷

Jefferson's model of checker-box wards of six miles square, embedded within counties that were, in turn, embedded within states was not offered due to any manic penchant for geographical neatness on his part. The proposal was part of Jefferson's attempt to maintain the revolutionary core of the national polity. Jefferson thought that a system of local government, organized into geographically concise units, was central to the survival of the republic, through which we could avoid a recurring need for violent revolution. This idea of the ward republic, although never coming to fruition, is embedded within the soul of American government as local government scholars Parris Glendenning and Mavis Mann Reeves have observed:

> The well-known Jeffersonian concept of "grass roots" government run by the people—miniature republics—has firmly taken hold in the American mind, "Self-government," "rural America," "the government closest to the people," "neighborhood government," and "grass roots democracy," are all terms repeated and defended daily, affirming America's commitment to small local units that can float with considerable autonomy on the turbulent seas of local government.⁹⁸

Certainly, Glendening and Reeves are correct about the latent influence of Jefferson's ward republic idea on American political culture. However, they do not go far enough. Jefferson did not understand his own ward proposal as something that would guarantee local autonomy. Jefferson, in fact, says very little about local autonomy in reference to the ward system. The wards were to be anything but autonomous. The wards were to be part of a seamless fabric that would keep the republic bundled close to its animating principles. No unit in Jefferson's system was autonomous. Both Jefferson and Adams understood the fundamental importance of local government in light of its position within the whole of the American regime. Neither Jefferson nor Adams praise local government apart from the greater context of the health of the republic, be it in the Revolution itself, the recurring revolution, or in some particular controversy. Granted, Jefferson ascribes to ward systems an almost millennial quality, one that is implicit in Adams' account of local government as well. Adams, in his own way, sees the New England towns as being sanctified by the Revolution. The New England towns had been cleansed, in a fundamental sense, of their previous defects. For both Adams and Jefferson, there is a providential quality to local government and the American Founding, a quality that would have been readily understood by the Puritans when they conceived of building in America a "city upon a hill."

Conclusion

The American Founders were keen to connect the health of local politics with the health of the overall regime. If this connection is not maintained, local liberty merely becomes local autonomy, the freedom for a town to do what it thinks is best. As we saw in our examination of Puritan rule in Massachusetts, town freedom could often mean the destruction of liberty, as the Founders understood the concept. Hence, the Founders reinterpret the concept of local government in a fundamental fashion. The locality exists for the sake of the overall regime.

Local residents must be alive to questions of greater significance. In this way, the agitation that can be caused by local governments can affect political issues of wider scope. The more active the local governments are in these issues, the more difficult it will be for authorities in central governments to engage in despotism. Local questions cannot be separated from the greater issues of a republic. Local government is important in that it provides a political gateway for the citizen to the overall politics of the regime. The more structured the local system, the easier it is for this role of the local citizenry to take shape. The more confused and decentralized the structure, the harder it is for local citizens to have the desired effect on national politics. Adams praised New England local governments, in addition to their competent provision of public services, for their forbearance in momentous political struggles. Jefferson praised the New England towns for this as well, even when their success came at his expense. And Jefferson lamented the lack of such a structure in the South and was worried about what would come of the nation if the New England system was not, in some way, implemented on a wide scale in America. We must bear in mind that it was not necessarily the system of New England government that we inherited from the colonial period that the Founders were keen to produce. Adams and Jefferson desired a new system of New England town government, one fit for a republic and devoted to the protection of natural rights.

❋ ❋ ❋

1. Patrick Henry, "Speeches of Patrick Henry in the Virginia Ratifying Convention," in *The Complete Anti-Federalist*, vol. 5, ed. Herbert Storing with assistance by Murray Dry (Chicago: University of Chicago Press, 1981), 224.
2. Thomas Jefferson, *The Writings of Thomas Jefferson*, vol. 15, ed.

Albert Ellery Bergh (Washington, DC: The Thomas Jefferson Memorial Association, 1907), 34. The Anti-Federalist Agrippa touts the sheriff as an office that had put down several insurrections within the colonies and states. Agrippa, "Letter II," in *The Complete Anti-Federalist*, vol. 4, 72.

3. James Wilson, *Works*, vol. 2, 461.
4. Ibid., 462.
5. George Washington, *The Writings of George Washington*, vol. 34, ed. John C. Fitzpatrick (Washington, DC: United States Government Printing Office, 1931), 123.
6. James Madison, *The Papers of James Madison*, vol. 8, eds. Robert A. Rutland, William M. E. Rachal, Barbara D. Ripel, and Fredrika J. Teute (Chicago: University of Chicago Press, 1973), 205.
7. Ibid., 206, n. 1. Sheriffs were protected from failing to collect taxes in 1783 due to "the scarcity of money and other circumstances."
8. Thomas Jefferson, *Papers of Thomas Jefferson*, vol. 1, eds. Julian P. Boyd and Lyman H. Butterfield (Princeton, NJ: Princeton University Press, 1950), 342, 350, 361. For a further analysis by Jefferson of the Virginia county court system see *Notes on the State of Virginia*, Introduction and Notes, William Peden (Chapel Hill: University of North Carolina Press, 1955), 130-149.
9. John Adams, *Diary and Autobiography of John Adams*, vol. 1, eds. L. H. Butterfield, Leonard C. Faber, and Wendell D. Garrett (Cambridge, MA: Harvard University Press, 1961), 135.
10. Ibid., 134-135.
11. Ibid., 136.
12. John Adams, *The Works of John Adams*, vol. 4, 192, 198, 207.
13. Benjamin Franklin, *Benjamin Franklin's Autobiography*, eds. J. A. Leo Lemay and P. M. Zall (New York: W.W. Norton and Company, 1986), 86.
14. Ibid.
15. Ibid. Franklin went on to serve as a Justice of the Peace and as a representative in the Pennsylvania legislature, in addition to serving on several independent commissions in Philadelphia.
16. Jefferson, *Notes*, 165.
17. Jefferson, "Letter to Dr. Benjamin Rush," September 23, 1800, *Writings*, vol. 10, 173.
18. See Harry V. Jaffa, *The Conditions of Freedom* (Baltimore: Johns Hopkins University Press, 1975), 99-110.

19. Jefferson, *Writings*, vol. 10, 173.
20. Ibid., 429.
21. Ibid., 431.
22. Adams, *Diary*, vol. 1, 205.
23. Ibid., 136.
24. Joseph S. Wood, *The New England Village*, with a contribution by Michael P. Steinitz (Baltimore: Johns Hopkins University, 1997), 44.
25. Ibid., 2.
26. Joseph S. Wood, "Build Therefore Your Own World: The New England Village as Settlement Ideal," *Annals of the Association of American Geographers* 81, no. 1 (1991), 41-42. Plymouth, MA, Salem, MA, and Hampton, NH were other examples of nucleated settlements that had formed in the colonial period. Wood, *New England Village*, 46. See also David Grayson Allen, *In English Ways* (Chapel Hill, NC: University of North Carolina Press, 1981), 8.
27. Wood, "Build Therefore Your Own World," 36.
28. Ibid., 37, 39, 48.
29. Ibid., 32.
30. Wood, *New England Village*, 11.
31. From W. T. Davis, *History of the Town of Plymouth* (NY: Charles Scribner and Sons, 1921), 253, in Wood, *New England Village*, 44.
32. C. F. Adams, *Three Episodes*, 610.
33. Wood, "Build," 32.
34. Wood, *Village*, 180.
35. Wood, "Build," 34, 52.
36. Wood, *Village*, 64.
37. Wood, "Build," 35.
38. C. F. Adams, *Episodes*, 783.
39. Adams, *Diary*, vol. 1, 128.
40. C. F. Adams, *Episodes*, 686-687.
41. Adams, *Diary*, vol. 1, 129.
42. Ibid., 191.
43. C. F. Adams, *Episodes*, 790.
44. Ibid., 793.
45. Adams, *Diary*, vol. 1, 82-83.

46. Ibid., 82.
47. Ibid., 96.
48. *Diary*, vol. 3, 279. Adams suspects that he was nominated as surveyor by a friend, Dr. Savil, so that Adams would be exempt from serving as constable. A constable collected town taxes and was held financially responsible for uncollected revenue. The office had ruined many of its holders.
49. C. F. Adams, *Episodes*, 675-676; Adams, *Diary*, vol. 1, 203; Adams, *Diary*, vol. 3, 278-279.
50. David McCullough, *John Adams* (New York: Simon and Schuster, 2001), 48-49.
51. C. F. Adams, *Episodes*, 790.
52. Bruce C. Daniels, *Dissent and Conformity*, 92.
53. Carl Bridenbaugh, *Cities in Revolt*, 7; Robert E. Brown, *Middle-Class Democracy and the Revolution*, 98; Richard D. Brown, *Revolutionary Politics in Massachusetts*, 5.
54. Anne Bush Maclear, *Early New England Towns*, 107. See also Ellen Elizabeth Callahan, *Hadley: A Study of the Political Development of a Typical New England Town*, 13.
55. Bruce C. Daniels, *The Connecticut Town*, 81. Daniels, *Dissent and Conformity*, 100. However, as Daniels notes, meeting frequency would rise during crises. And Boston, for example, retained the town meeting until 1822. William O. Winter, *State and Local Government in a Decentralized Republic*, 22.
56. Daniels, *Dissent and Conformity*, 98.
57. Charles M. Andrews, *The River Towns*, 53; Daniels, *Dissent*, 92; David Syrett, "Town Meeting Politics in Massachusetts," 355.
58. Alexis de Tocqueville, *Democracy in America*, 57.
59. Ibid., 64.
60. Ibid., 65.
61. Ibid., 56.
62. *The Federalist Papers*, 49.
63. Ibid., 52.
64. Bruce C. Daniels, "Introduction," in *Town and County: Essays*, ed. Bruce C. Daniels, 10.
65. C. F. Adams, *Episodes*, 790.
66. Emphasis added. John Adams, *Works*, vol. 3, 400.

67. C. F. Adams, *Episodes*, 783.
68. Ibid., 783-784.
69. Adams, *Diary*, vol. 1, 263.
70. Adams, *Works*, vol. 5, 494.
71. Ibid., 494-495.
72. Emphasis added. Patrick Henry, "Speeches of Patrick Henry in the Virginia Ratifying Convention," 243-244.
73. James Madison, *Letters and Other Writings of James Madison*, vol. 1 (New York: R. Worthington, 1884), 181-182.
74. Adams, *Works*, vol. 7, 168.
75. Ibid., 182-183.
76. Hannah Arendt, *On Revolution* (New York: Viking Press, 1963), 252.
77. Jefferson, *Writings*, vol. 12, 393-394.
78. Adams, *Works*, vol. 7, 182-183.
79. Jefferson, *Writings*, vol. 13, 399-400.
80. Jefferson, *Writings*, vol. 16, 46.
81. Jefferson, *Writings*, vol. 15, 38.
82. Jefferson, *Writings*, vol. 12, 393-394.
83. Jefferson, *Writings*, vol. 13, 399-400.
84. Arendt, *On Revolution*, 252.
85. Ibid., 253.
86. Jefferson, *Writings*, vol. 14, 70.
87. Ibid., 421.
88. Arendt, *On Revolution*, 254.
89. Jefferson, *Writings*, vol. 15, 43.
90. Jefferson, *Writings*, vol. 14, 421-422.
91. Victor Davis Hanson, *The Soul of Battle* (New York: Free Press, 1999); Victor Davis Hanson, *The Western Way of War* (Berkeley, CA: University of California Press, 2000).
92. Jefferson, *Writings*, vol. 12, 393-394.
93. Jean M. Yarbrough, *American Virtues: Thomas Jefferson on the Character of a Free People* (Lawrence, KS: University of Kansas Press, 1998), 133.
94. Ibid., 135.

95. Richard Matthews, *The Radical Politics of Thomas Jefferson* (Lawrence, KS: University of Kansas Press, 1984), 16.

96. Michael P. Zuckert, *The Natural Rights Republic* (Notre Dame, IN: University of Notre Dame Press, 1996), 236.

97. Ibid., 243.

98. Parris N. Glendenning and Mavis Mann Reeves, *Pragmatic Federalism*, 295.

Chapter Four

ALL LOCAL POLITICS IS NATIONAL

While colonial local government was often decentralized, it was in no sense anarchic. Colonial governments set forth clear guidelines for town authority, in which the local residents of some colonies enjoyed a great measure of influence. Little of the confusion regarding lines of authority that plagues our modern system of local government existed in colonial North America. The most ardent proponent of strong local institutions was arguably Thomas Jefferson, and the reforms he proposed entailed the creation of a nationwide network of wards that would allow direct citizen participation in government. These wards would exist within a highly structured system that included county and state governments, along with the national government. Jefferson's observations cannot be cast off as merely the musings of a radical Republican, for the observations on local government by Federalist John Adams were almost identical to those of Jefferson.

As we have seen, Adams and Jefferson thought that local government, properly understood, served as an important line of defense against the despotic pretensions of central authorities. This defense could be effective only if the local governments themselves possessed authority and a political structure clearly delineated and easily understood by the average citizen. That is, both Adams and Jefferson saw local government as useful in the defense of republican government provided it was highly structured. It should come as no surprise today when we find that state and national governments have come to dominate local governments as the structure of those local entities has become less defined.

Adams and Jefferson understood local government as fulfilling a vital role in the overall maintenance of the republic. In addition to their role as providers of necessary day-to-day services, local governments were also important for their role in controversies that went beyond local issues. One of the great purposes of local government, according to Adams and Jefferson, was its role in sustaining the republic. The republic was not made for the purpose of sustaining local government. And, most certainly, local government was not made merely to sustain local government itself.

Certainly, the principles of natural right expressed by the Founders have implications for the conduct of local governments: property rights, protection of religious liberty, and free trade, among others. However, if the nation in which such localities exist ceases to be guided by natural right principles, local liberty will be difficult to maintain. Accordingly, the Founders devoted much of their concern to the broader role of local government, one that perhaps reveals its true nature. Local government provides a political gateway for the citizen and allows him to view the entire field of republican government in a federal system: national, state, and local. It is his first point of contact with the regime. In fact, local politics provide a gateway for the citizen to enter the field of politics in general, if politics is understood in its most fundamental sense.

Prior to the September 11 attacks, it may have been difficult for modern Americans to recognize the role of local government as something other than the medium through which day-to-day services are provided. However, with the late realization that localities could, at any time, become the frontlines of the War on Terror, the other and often forgotten role is becoming increasingly evident. Public danger has crystallized for us the full nature of our political institutions. Civil society can dissolve—for minutes, hours, days, months—in the instant a suicide bomber, mass murderer, or hurricane wreaks deadly havoc. Our examination of the history of colonial local government—the context within which key Founders made their observations—and the writings of key Founders themselves reveal that they had access to this extreme local experience. In the colonial period, local political units carried out the core functions of government in the most severe situations.

Local institutions, like the town meeting, were regularly forced into action when colonial and royal governments were unable to respond. The New England town meeting, for example, was not a superior instrument of a democratic polity because it shaped the human soul and trained the citizen in the arts of deliberation. The reality of the town meeting was a sobering reminder that the state of nature was ever-present. It was up to the meetings' attendants to make, at times, life and death decisions, and to exercise political power in its most fundamental form. This was clear to colonists who lived with the dread reality of attack by hostile forces, disease, or natural disasters. It has also become clearer to us in the present, given recent events.

Local governments, properly understood, are not simply the janitors of the republic. They are also the sentinels of the republic. One of the most important lessons learned from an examination of the colonial experience is that the colonists and some significant Founders saw both functions as a vital and natural role of local government. This is not to say that local administration is unimportant, quite the contrary. However, the thoughts of key Founders on the issue of local government point us toward a richer understanding of local government as a vital political entity in American life.

The lessons in the previous chapters point us toward a radical reevaluation of local government. Local government is the most basic and ancient political institution. As previously stated, both James Wilson (Federalist) and George Bryan (Anti-Federalist) understood the American system of local government as one derived from Saxon government, although one could conceivably trace the roots of local government to the first time two or more human beings entered upon a common course of action. The Saxons created a local government structure with which we would be familiar today, comprising counties, towns, and villages. However, Wilson and Bryan did not employ the ethnic mysticism used by Herbert Baxter Adams when describing the origins of local government. Bryan, writing in 1776 under the pen-name Demophilus, argued that the Saxons were exercising their natural rights when they formed their local units of government. A people could appeal to these rights regardless of ethnicity, and Bryan offers his readers the example of the American Indians' use of direct local government: "It is from the prevalence of this custom among the savages, that they have been enabled to astonish our great lawyers, judges and governors, commissioned to treat with them, by displays of their sublime policy."[1] While his use of the term "savages" may strike us today as coarse, Bryan most certainly holds the American Indian, in principle, as equal to the Saxons in their genuine human desire for free institutions. James Wilson, writing in 1790, concurs with Bryan's analysis of the origins of local government. He describes the early Saxons as existing in a state of nature: "When the Saxons first settled in Britain, they found themselves obliged, by the disorders of the times, to associate, in their different settlements, for their mutual security and protection....These societies were known by the appellation of vills or towns."[2]

Thomas Jefferson, however, departs slightly from the analyses of Bryan and Wilson. In a letter to John Cartwright written in 1824, Jefferson agrees with his correspondent that the English system of government was derived from the Saxons: "Your derivation of [the English Constitution] from the Anglo-Saxons, seems to be made on legitimate principles."[3] But Jefferson then distinguishes the American experience from that of the ancient Saxons:

> Our Revolution commenced on more favorable ground. It presented us an album on which we were free to write what we pleased. We had no occasion to search into musty records, to hunt up royal parchments, or to investigate the laws and institutions of a semi-barbarous ancestry. We appealed to those of nature, and found them engraved in our hearts.[4]

Local Government: The Fundamentals

From Bryan, Jefferson, and Wilson we have an image of local government in its most fundamental condition. Even if the more sophisticated elements of civil society were to fall apart, local government in some form will survive. In a state of nature, local government will be the only remnant of political life, even if local government devolves to the basic unit of the household. It is from this perspective that the Founders who analyzed local government encourage us to think of the full meaning of local political life.

Local government is important because it is always there. Properly understood, it is within the consideration of the true condition of local government that the state of nature reveals itself to us as something real. The state of nature is an ever-present possibility. From our examination of colonial experience and the thoughts of Adams and Jefferson in the previous chapters, it does not appear that local institutions are as much an instrument to shape the human soul as much as they are a reminder of the precarious condition of political life. The role of local government, understood by Adams, Jefferson, and other Founders, is not simply that of a potential instrument of revolution.

Local governments can become the effective government at anytime. In the age of modern terrorism and the threat of nuclear war, local governments live with the possibility of being thrust into a state of nature.[5] In this light we can reconsider Alexander Hamilton's statement from *The Federalist* 17 below:

> Upon the same principle that a man is more attached to his family than to his neighborhood, to his neighborhood than to the community at large, the people of each State would be apt to feel a stronger bias towards their local governments than towards the government of the Union; unless the force of that principle should be destroyed by a much better administration of the latter.[6]

This is true, of course, as long as the higher levels of government remain intact or able to respond to local crises. An appreciation of this situation reveals the essence of local government. Through such an understanding, we are hearkened back to the most fundamental understanding of political life. We are reminded that political life has tragic elements. As was true for our colonial forebearers, we live constantly on the edge of civil society's collapse. While bridge repair, road construction, urban redevelopment, and the like are the objects of local government, its substance is something altogether different. This is perhaps one reason the Founders made similar arguments when writing about local government. In an extreme situation, most would be in agreement that survival becomes paramount. If all terrorism is, in the end, local, then, we have a better appreciation for the true meaning of the old phrase that "all politics is local."[7]

The devotees of the administrative state do not understand local government in this way. By ignoring the natural right tradition, they lose touch with the ever-present possibility of a return to the state of nature. It is not part of the plan of History. They cannot account for the fact that their historicism is, itself, historically grounded and could be shattered at any time by a suicide bomb, serial sniper, mass murderer, nuclear bomb, or hurricane. The Founders had access to this experience. In the American Revolution, local political units carried on the core functions of government in the most extreme situations.

In our previous chapters, the examination of local government ended, for each colony, with the onset of the Revolution. This was more than a utilitarian construction; it was a necessary device to give us the proper context in which the Founders examined local institutions. It also reveals the nature of local government more clearly. Both Adams and Jefferson understood local government not only as the Revolution-in-potential but as politics-in-potential. Given Adams' low opinion of town morals and town politics, it should be shocking to us that Adams then praises the New England town as one of the four vital institutions that contributed to the success of the Revolution. Adams did not have any higher opinions of local life, understood as such, after the Revolution than he did before. But he did praise the New England towns.

The lesson from Adams is that politics—true politics—is an ever-present possibility and human beings, no matter how far they may have temporarily fallen, do have a nature that can allow them to respond properly should the need arise. For Adams, local political life is, even when it descends into corruption, redeemable. The moral climate of a locality is no doubt important for the full realization of a proper human life. Yet towns with a debauched civic character may indeed rise to the occasion when called upon. In fact, the proper recognition of the ultimate responsibility of local government may make the more venal forms of local corruption less common. The character of a town, as Adams' thoughts on the matter suggest, may improve only after a confrontation with this brute reality.

The received opinion as to the lessons of Tocqueville leads us in another direction. An immersion into the murky pools of town politics may not be the best practice to bring true civic virtue to the fore. Americans, now and then, can be virtuous in spite of town politics, not because of them. The true "political" character of a locality may have little to do with town "politics." Tocqueville may have had it all wrong. Tocqueville may have been too focused on the emotional quality of town participation as a training ground for the soul.

The Founders who spoke most extensively on local government understood that those governments might one day again be forced to become *the* regime or the vessel through which the regime survives. Its position is important. Local government is less important for its formative qualities, as is suggested by a certain reading of Tocqueville. Rather, local government, properly understood in light of the American Founding, is not something that will "become" a certain thing, good or bad. It is something that simply "is." Our struggle is to remain ever mindful of its presence. Adams was disgusted with local politics *qua* local. Such a man would no doubt be restless with the forgetfulness that comes with a temporary peace. People return to their drams, their tobacco, and their struggle with private temptations.

This is not to say that a life of leisure is a false life. This is just to say that, to a man like Adams, it must have all seemed silly in light of what could be and, in fact, what was to become of New England in her struggle against the Crown. Adams saw the towns come alive during the Stamp Act crisis. The towns led the struggle. The towns, in effect, became the government. Local government was redeemed. Its fundamental nature was revealed. Both Adams and Jefferson are in lock step on this point.

New Englanders did not fight for abstract rights of local autonomy. Appeals for local government autonomy, understood as such, can perhaps be understood as either appeals to postmodern ideology—moral relativism leading to a perverse popular sovereignty to do exactly what one pleases, regardless of the consequences—or to a pre-monotheistic understanding of political life—each city with its own gods and ways of life. Local government in a natural right republic reveals its character when it acts as medium through which a full political life can reveal itself. This is what Jefferson saw in the New England town during the Embargo Act controversy. He admired the local governments for their resistance to this policy. And both Adams and Jefferson admired the New England towns for their persistence in seeing the Revolution through to its successful conclusion. Local governments were admired for specific actions in an actual crisis, not for demonstrating some abstract quality of autonomy.

The understanding of local government as the venue in which we can indulge our eclectic tastes for a unique experience is superficial. It is a luxury afforded to us by forgetfulness. Properly speaking there is a difference between local government as an element of American federalism and local government as the preservation of a *locale.*

American townsmen in the American Revolution fought for their natural rights. The towns were the media through which this struggle took place. And one vital element that allowed the New England towns to appreciate their true political character, was their recognition as the units upon which representation was based in the Massachusetts assembly. Local residents may more clearly see their true character if represented on such a basis in state legislatures. In fact, as we know from our examination of colonial government, every colony based its representation in the colonial assembly upon local units. As we know, even the great national architect, James Madison, saw local units as the proper basis upon which to affix representation in a state legislature. After the court rulings in *Baker v. Carr* (1962) and *Reynolds v. Sims* (1964), this element of a structured decentralization is no longer available to us.[8]

The power and importance of the New England town may have come less from the type and quality of community life than the simple fact that the colony of Massachusetts apportioned representatives by town, thus giving the town, as such, real political power. This factor, more than any other, may account for the importance of the town in New England and its subsequent role in the Revolution. Its position within the regime was crucial, not its formational quality with respect to the civic soul. Due to their ability to be represented in the assembly as local units, the New England towns may well have had that power even if their social communities were not as closely formed. Adams and Jefferson certainly did not see such deliberation as inherently glorious.

Your Land is My Land: Modern Examples of Despotic Local Government

Both Adams and Madison offer rather pointed remarks about local life. The business of local government, understood apart from the preservation of natural rights, was, at best, a necessarily tedious one and at worst a downright nasty business indeed. Given recent developments in local government, this business is getting nastier still.

Consider the 1981 case of the Poletown neighborhood in Detroit.[9] Poletown was a working-class neighborhood, which contained a mix of homes, businesses, churches, and a hospital.[10] By most accounts, the neighborhood was well-kept. The problem for those in Poletown was that General Motors wanted the area to be the site of a Cadillac assembly plant. General Motors wanted the city to destroy the neighborhood to make way for the plant. If the city failed to demolish the neighborhood, GM would take its business elsewhere. Many residents of the neighborhood joined in a lawsuit to stop the development, citing Fifth Amendment protections. Under the Fifth Amendment to the U.S. Constitution, the government can use eminent domain to take property so long as there will be a public use for the new project. The traditional understanding of public use had been the construction of roads, bridges, infrastructure, or government buildings.

But in *Berman v. Parker* (1954), the U.S. Supreme Court declared that "public use" also meant "public purpose."[11] The Court declared that the government could use eminent domain powers to renovate a "blighted" area of Washington, D.C. So, in addition to public use requirements, the aesthetic tastes and economic designs of civic officials could now factor into eminent domain decisions. As John Fund, a columnist for the *Wall Street Journal*, remarks, "It soon became clear that too often urban renewal really meant 'Negro Removal,' as cities increasingly razed stable neighborhoods to benefit powerful interests."[12]

In *Poletown Neighborhood Council v. Detroit* (1981) this logic was extended by the Michigan Supreme Court to justify the destruction of an ethnically diverse neighborhood that was not blighted. This was done in the name of the economic benefits that would accrue to the area. Thus, when the property rights of some are violated, as in *Berman*, soon the property rights of all may come under attack. The neighborhood was leveled and the auto plant was built. The Michigan Supreme Court eventually overturned the *Poletown* decision in 2004, but the neighborhood has long been destroyed.[13] Future property owners, in Michigan at least, may be spared the fate of Poletown. The Cadillac factory is still running, but it is arguable whether or not the economic benefits promised by General Motors and the City of Detroit have come to fruition.[14]

Perhaps emboldened by the *Poletown* case, officials in Cypress, California sought to invoke eminent domain authority to take property owned by a growing and dynamic evangelical church, the Cottonwood Christian Center. City officials wanted to take the land and give it to Costco. This taking was justified as a "public use," according to city officials because Costco would pay more taxes than the church. The Cypress plan was later struck down in federal district court.[15]

Violations of one's natural right to property do not come from eminent domain powers or development authorities alone. Modern zoning laws can also deprive property owners of their rights. It must be recognized that most people would not want a steel mill operating next to their home and, thus, might favor the general principle of zoning.

Modern zoning requirements, however, are becoming increasingly burdensome to property owners. According to columnist James Bovard, "If you want to use your own land, increasingly you have to beg, bribe, and grovel to the nearest government bureaucrat. Local zoning officials are increasingly petty dictators, ruling and ruining the lives of average citizens."[16] Consider the following examples.

Officials in Flosmoor, Illinois prohibited pickup trucks from being parked in streets or private driveways.[17] The town of Coral Gables, Florida, requires residents to pay a $35 permit in order to paint the *interior* of their homes. According to Bovard, "Local building inspectors patrol the streets looking for painting trucks parked at homes that have not paid the permit fee."[18] The city of Los Angeles forbids writers from practicing their craft in home offices in residential neighborhoods. The city of Chicago has a similar zoning law. In one case they issued a cease-and-desist order to prevent a couple from writing software and magazine articles out of their home office. The town of Carol Stream, Illinois, according to Bovard, "rigorously polices the roofs, windows, home colors, and building materials of homes to insure that they are not too similar or too dissimilar to their neighbors."[19] Bovard is quick to point out that the standards are vague and much discretion is left to local bureaucrats to engage in "spot zoning." Apparently, under these conditions, local officials can make up the rules as they go along.

Consider, furthermore, the case of a Princeton, New Jersey, shopkeeper who, under threat of a 90-day jail sentence, was required to remove barbecue grills on display outside his store. The shop owner had been displaying similar items outside of his store for over 50 years. A new zoning regulation, however, allowed only the display of books, flowers, plants, vegetables, and newspapers. In addition, consider the town of East Hampton, Long Island, which issued an arrest warrant for a shop owner who had stacked a few pumpkins outside of his store.[20] Apparently, the town ruled that the pumpkins amounted to a shop sign and the owner had not paid for a sign permit. And in the spirit of the city of Cypress, California, officials in Boston invoked historic preservation regulations to prevent a Catholic church from changing their windows, paint scheme, doors, and a painting depicting the Assumption of the Blessed Virgin Mary. According to Bovard, local officials thought they were justified "in proclaiming themselves pope."[21] Finally, in Fullerton, California, city officials were concerned about parking problems caused by an active and growing local evangelical church. The city's solution was to ban parking within two blocks of the church on Sunday morning from the hours of 8:00 am. to 12:00 pm.[22]

The denouement, perhaps, of the episodes mentioned above has come in the form of the Supreme Court's 5-4 decision in *Kelo v. New London* (2005).[23] The case involved a plan by Pfizer pharmaceuticals to build a research facility in a working-class neighborhood in New London, Connecticut. The New London city council delegated the task of organizing the development plan to the New London Development Corporation, a non-elected body. The development corporation selected a neighborhood to be demolished under eminent domain authority. Several homeowners in the area sued New London, arguing that the taking of their land in order to build a pharmaceutical facility violated the "public use" provisions in the Fifth Amendment. The Connecticut Supreme Court sided with the city and the Supreme Court of the United States upheld that decision.

The Supreme Court, according to Justice Sandra Day O'Connor, who dissented from the opinion, has made private property "vulnerable to being taken and transferred to another private owner, so long as it might be upgraded—i.e., given to an owner who will use it in a way that the legislature deems more beneficial to the public—in the process."[24] In fact, Justice O'Connor goes on to suggest that this decision opens the door for any eminent domain action a government may wish to pursue. In effect, a property owner is now at the mercy of local officials, no matter what the purpose of the proposed project may be. In short, if government officials think that a future owner may use a property in a more beneficial fashion, the present owner is helpless under the law. O'Connor continues: "For who among us can say she already makes the most productive or attractive possible use of her property? The specter of condemnation hangs over all property. Nothing is to prevent the State from replacing any Motel 6 with a Ritz-Carlton, any home with a shopping mall, or any farm with a factory."[25]

Justice O'Connor's comments have greater implications than a danger to property rights. A wary business owner may feel restrained in expressing opinions about incumbent politicians for fear that city officials may retaliate and take his property. What is to prevent city officials from "redeveloping" neighborhoods with voting patterns that are troublesome for incumbent office holders? Once the right to property is no longer secure, it is certain that threats to other rights will surely follow. Accordingly, it is not enough for us to wish that citizens more regularly participate in local affairs. We are well beyond the point where increased civic participation alone will yield results that will restore our natural liberties. In fact, as the *Kelo* case suggests, we must set our sights on larger matters in order to save our cities, towns, townships, and counties.

The trampling of our natural rights has come as a result of a long process. So-called Progressive standards of civic betterment, aesthetic tastes, and community development, apparently, have greater moral force today than the recognition of one's God-given rights to life, liberty, and the pursuit of happiness. And, as we have attempted to show, property rights cannot be separated from the enjoyment of other rights.

Local politics are important. In today's context, however, local politics must serve as a starting point for citizens to take back their nation and restore the preeminent authority of natural right principles. This may involve a return to an understanding of local government as held by the Founders. Citizens must understand the true nature of local government and its ability to participate in issues of wider scope. In order to save the community, we may have to fight on a political battleground that lies beyond our immediate localities. Under the conditions set forth by *Kelo*, the "community" may be irreparably damaged. Change must come from the outside.

With respect to the perceived importance of local participation, deliberations about town administration and government can be beneficial if that deliberation is understood as a means by which natural rights are protected. The recognition of an individual's natural right to life, liberty, and property, however, is the recognition of the ultimate responsibility that each person has with respect to the ever-possible return of the state of nature. That is, one encounters great difficulty when the conditions for a proper civic life are set so that local commerce must be conducted in a soulfully glorious fashion. Unless animated by the principles of natural rights, intense deliberation about zoning regulations, eminent domain, or redevelopment will not replenish the soul nor make one a bold opponent of tyranny. Such deliberations are just as likely to make one an inert object within the great machine, going through the motions within the vast administrative state, a party to the crime.

Community?

Local government is the smallest unit of government. It is basic. If society were to disintegrate, there might not be a national government, there might not be state governments, but there will always be local governments. The proper understanding of local government makes us aware of the tragic quality of political life. That tragedy is always there, waiting to happen.

In the age of global terrorism this idea is accessible to us today, as it was for the Founders, who brought about a world-historical event. This has very little to do with how much control a local city council has over their pension funds or other such necessities. There must be local officials in place who can act if an extreme situation arises, like the Greek yeoman who could make the quick transition from his private affairs to the defense of the *polis* and take his place in the phalanx.[26] Rudy Giuliani is known as the "Mayor of America" for good reason. This is not to mention the regard with which the New York police and firefighters have been held after the September 11 attacks, a regard that has been projected onto police and firefighters throughout the nation. Jefferson, in his description of his ward republics, alludes to imagery like this, as does Adams in his description of the qualities of the New England town that most contributed to the success of the Revolution.

This is the nature of local government. It is always there. Yet we, understandably, choose not to focus upon it. It is difficult for the modern man, surrounded by comfort, distraction, and constant motion to think that his life could be anything other than a transition from one comfort to the next. Forgetfulness sustains itself on frenetic behavior. Thus, the more thoughtful person becomes, properly so, concerned about the dearth of community feeling in modern local life. We are too busy "bowling alone" to be concerned with civic participation.[27]

One is left to wonder whether or not we are too obsessed with the creation of "community." But when the tragic nature of human life once again rears its head, the community will most likely reappear. We should not glory in tragedy for the sake of the community feeling it brings, nor perhaps should we lament the loss of community in the absence of tragedy. Both are always there, although one or the other may be dormant at any given time. It appears that the New Englanders of the colonial period loved their private life just as much as we do, although there is no denying that our electronically-devised distractions are far more dangerous and ubiquitous. But, as of yet, we are not altogether different than our colonial political ancestors. New York City, with its many distractions, responded to the September 11 attacks with a vigor that was comparable to any of the great civic efforts in American history.

The community is there if we need it. To deny this is to deny, perhaps, that there is a human nature with an eternal quality. Thus, our efforts to create community might be found, in the end, to be a wasted effort. We may not want to focus so much on the creation of community as we should on the elimination of barriers to its formation should the need arise. The structure of the various local governments must be clear enough to provide the best opportunity for this reemergence to occur. In other words, we should be less concerned with creating community and more concerned about whether or not we are standing in its way by devising schemes of local government that are designed more to confuse than to clarify.

In the age of global terrorism this is easier for us to see. We have an insight into local government and the American Founding that was perhaps harder for us to see in the recent past. The administrative state is a danger because the Progressives taught us that all life is administration, i.e. business. And the business of life can be made perfect through the organizational decrees of modern social science. According to the Progressives, we need to make government more like business and business more like government.[28] This peculiar understanding of life, however, makes us less aware of the tragic nature of life and it may make us potentially helpless in the face of such tragedy. When tragedy comes calling, with whom would we be most comfortable as the agent of our immediate safety—Tocqueville's deliberative townsman, Woodrow Wilson's professional administrator, or John Adams' tobacco-smoking, dram-drinking, musket-carrying rustic? The attempt over the past century and a half to drive the "rustic" from the town square may satisfy our prudery but it may come at a high price.[29]

Conservatives, Liberals, and Local Politics

John Adams and Thomas Jefferson saw local government—from both the colonial experience and its role in the future of America—as important in light of its contribution to creating and sustaining a polity devoted to the preservation of natural rights. All of the activity of local government, be it mundane or grand, was judged in this light. For both of these great Founders, local governments achieved their apotheoses in struggles involving principles and issues of a wider scope. As mentioned in the Introduction to this work, local government, according to Adams and Jefferson, was made for the republic. The republic was not made for the purpose of sustaining local government. And, most certainly, local government was not made to sustain local government itself. In this respect, those on the Progressive Left have a better grasp of the essence of local government than do modern American conservatives. While not animated by the same principles that Adams and Jefferson recognized, modern liberals appear to be more aware of the important role that local government has in our federal system—the provider of life's mundane necessities and the *provocateur* of grand revolutions. The liberals, while motivated by the historicism of the modern administrative state, have more clearly held to the true understanding of local government as a political entity in full.

In Table 4.1 we see a depiction of local government activity with respect to issues that are not normally associated with municipal affairs. A LexisNexis search was conducted on the "U.S. News" database for all four regions listed in this data base: Midwestern, Northeastern, Southeastern, and Western. A search was conducted for articles dating two years prior to March 1, 2005. Articles containing the terms "city council" and "resolution" were examined, with a Boolean operator on the latter term triggering a response if it occurred within ten words of the former. There were 88 articles on city councils taking action on issues beyond the normal scope of municipal administration and government. The total number of resolutions in the table is 85. Some articles mentioned more than one resolution and some mentioned one that had been the subject of another article.

While local governments made their voice heard in support of American troops, the bulk of local government activity in this sample can clearly be identified as being conducted by the Left. Outrage over the Patriot Act is clearly the dominant category within the data set, with support for the troops coming in at a distant second place. Support for so-called same-sex marriage is the next most frequent category of activity. Opposition to the Iraq War registers as the fourth most numerous category.

Table 4.1 City Council Resolutions, Non-Binding, Non-Municipal, 2003-2005

PATRIOT ACT, AGAINST (31)

* Los Angeles, CA
* Lincoln, NE
* Amers, IA
* Carbondale, IL
* Chicago, IL
* Ann Arbor, MI
* Minneapolis, MN
* Madison, WI
* Lowell, MA
* Albany, NY
* Schenectady, NY
* Paterson, NJ
* Pittsburgh, PA
* Portland, ME
* New York, NY
* Providence, RI
* Raleigh, NC
* Aspen, CO
* Olympia, WA
* Sacramento, CA
* Boise, ID
* Bayard, NM
* Austin, TX
* San Ramon, CA
* Albuquerque, NM
* Tonasket, WA
* Hayward, CA
* South Pasadena, CA
* Philadelphia, PA
* Mill Valley, CA

TROOPS, SUPPORT FOR (12)

* Vergennes, VT
* Los Angeles, CA
* Columbia, VA
* Cheyenne, WO
* Tualatin, OR
* Fresno, CA
* Santa Fe, NM
* Camarillo, CA
* Oceanside, CA
* San Diego, CA
* Spokane, WA
* Airway Heights, WA

SAME SEX MARRIAGE, FOR (9)

* Ann Arbor, MI
* Madison, WI
* Charlottesville, VA
* Takoma Park, MD
* Los Angeles, CA
* Eugene, OR
* Aspen, CO
* Oakland, CA
* Davis, CA

Iraq War, Against (5)
* New York, NY
* Ely, MN
* Pittsburgh, PA.
* Mount Rainier, MD
* Rocklin, CA

God is the Basis of U.S. Heritage (4)
* Elizabeth City, VA
* Kinston, NC
* Clinton, TN
* Kennesaw, GA

Illegal Immigrant Rights (4)
* Providence, RI
* Watsonville, CA
* Albuquerque, NM
* Los Angeles, CA

Hate Crimes, Against (3)
* Chicago, IL
* Sacramento, CA
* Lathrop, CA

Bush Admn., For Impeachment (2)
* Arcata, CA
* Santa Cruz, CA

Waterways, Protect (2)
* Milwaukee, WI
* Mandeville, LA

Brown v. Board, Reaffirm Support
* Topeka, KN

Confederate Battle Flag, Against
* Savannah, GA

Rachel Corey Death, Investigation
* Berkeley, CA

Sadam Hussein, Against
* Los Angeles, CA

SAME-SEX MARRIAGE, AGAINST
*   Citrus Heights, CA

DISTASTEFUL MAGAZINE COVERS, AGAINST
*   Layton, UT

SLAVE REPARATIONS, FOR
*   Pine Bluff, AR

GUN INDUSTRY, AGAINST
*   Pittsburgh, PA

UNIVERSAL HEALTH CARE, FOR
*   Portland, ME

HALLOWEEN, INAPPROPRIATE ON SUNDAY
*   Chattanooga, TN

U.S. W.W. II POW'S, REPARATIONS FOR
*   Chicago, Il

MEDICAL MARIJUANA, FOR
*   Madison, WI

CORPORATION, NOT A "PERSON"
*   Berkeley, CA

Source: LexisNexis® News Search, U.S. News: Midwestern, Northeastern, Southeastern, and Western regions. The search was conducted for articles dating two years prior to March 1, 2005. Articles containing the terms "city council" and "resolution" were examined, with a Boolean operator on the latter term triggering a response if it occurred within ten words of the former. The total number of articles retrieved in this search was 1,511. Of these, there were 88 articles on city council resolutions of a non-binding, non-municipal character. The total number of resolutions in the table is 85. Some articles mentioned more than one resolution and some mentioned one that had been the subject of another article.

There appears to have been some activity—in the South—in response to the recent controversy over the public display of the Ten Commandments and the controversy over the invocation of God in the Declaration of Independence. These resolutions had the same frequency as those calling for the recognition of rights for illegal aliens. In addition, there were other various resolutions, some not clearly identified with either a liberal or conservative position. Interestingly, there were two city councils that called for the impeachment of top officials in the Bush administration while only one city council identified Saddam Hussein as a malevolent influence in the world.

It appears as if conservatives have accepted the Progressive notion that the business of local government is, in fact just that—business—understood as the mere administration of things. This is not to deny the proper role of commerce in a regime based upon natural rights principles. But one wonders whether conservatives are merely fighting a series of rearguard actions with respect to the preservation of those principles, not only in areas such as property rights and religious freedom, but in a wide variety of issues related to the preservation of a natural rights republic. There are, no doubt, thousands of local governments in the United States—be they counties, cities, towns, or townships—that are controlled by what may generally be described as conservatives. Yet, in our data set, we do not see a raft of resolutions decrying the regulatory abuses of the administrative state against property rights, the redefinition of the institution of marriage, and the activities of the modern abortion industry. There appears to be some evidence of activity—albeit located primarily in the South—with respect to the preservation of our religious heritage. And there appears to be a reservoir of local support for our troops fighting abroad. But it appears to be the case that modern conservatives, by and large, do not fully recognize that such vigorous local activism by liberals may create an environment in which the climate of opinion moves issues away from them, such as we witnessed in the 2006 mid-term elections and the 2008 presidential election. The silence of conservative local officials could be interpreted as acquiescence. On issues of national significance, in which our Founders saw a vital role for local government, conservatives are politically outmanned and outgunned. Conservatives should reassess their apparent rejection of the principles of local government and the American Founding.

Conclusion

Conservatives today do not appreciate the broader role of local politics that ordered the colonists' actions. Perhaps conservatives are captivated by a particular understanding of Tocqueville's teachings, one focused upon the idea of participation in and deliberation about local politics *qua* local. Participation is not sufficient for a conservative in today's moral-political environment. The conservative who desires to participate in local politics is at a particular disadvantage in an era dominated by an administrative state insistent on advancing the causes of moral nihilism, coercive regulation, and simple-minded multi-culturalism. Liberals are better equipped to enter this debate because the current spirit of the regime is more in line with their notion of what a polity ought to be. Their activity, thus, may be more effortless, given the ground on which they are required to act.

Conservatives have a more difficult time in this environment. In order to overcome this, they must first transform the current understanding of local politics and more fully appreciate the lessons of colonial experience and the teachings of the American Founders. They must see local politics not as a medium through which they can more fully connect with the community but instead as a gateway to change the rules of the regime in which they operate. They must focus on the broader picture instead of simply willing themselves to participate more fully in a game whose rules have been written by those on the Left. Enhanced activity alone will not change the trajectory upon which the American regime is tending. The rules have been set-up so that conservatives will lose. The 2005 *Kelo* decision is just one example in a long train of abuses by the administrative state. If they desire to succeed, conservatives must change the rules by focusing on the regime generally. Local politics provides the conservative with an entry point at which he or she may begin to rewrite those rules.

❋ ❋ ❋

1. George Bryan, "The Genuine Principles of the Ancient Saxon, or English, Constitution," in *American Political Writing*, 349.
2. James Wilson, *Works*, vol. 2, 448.
3. Thomas Jefferson, *The Writings of Thomas Jefferson*, vol. 16, 42.
4. Ibid., 44.
5. See Joel Kotkin, "City Of the Future: Unless it keeps its citizens safe, the modern metropolis may go the way of ancient Rome," *Washington Post*, 24 July 2005, B 1.
6. *The Federalist Papers*, 87.
7. Thomas "Tip" O'Neill, *All Politics is Local, and Other Rules of the Game* (Cincinnati, OH: Adams Media Corporation, 1995); See also R. P. Eddy, "In the End All Terrorism is Local," *The Times* (London), 8 July 2005: edition 3WC, 24.
8. *Baker v. Carr* 369 US 186 (1962); *Reynolds v. Simms* 377 US 533 (1964).
9. *Poletown Neighborhood Council v. Detroit* 410 Mich. 616, 304 N.W. 2d 455 (1981).
10. See Steven Greenhut, "Property Rights Not Just a Defense for the Rich," *Tulsa World* (Oklahoma), 15 Aug. 2004, G4.

11. *Berman v. Parker* 348 US 26; 75 S. Ct. 98; 99 L. Ed. 27; (1954).
12. John Fund, "Property Rights are Civil Rights," *Opinion Journal (Wall Street Journal)*, 11 July 2005 < http://www.opinionjournal.com/diary/?id = 110006941 > (Accessed 29 July 2005).
13. *County of Wayne v. Hathcock* 471 Mich. 445; N.W. 2d 765 (2004).
14. See Greenhut, "Property Rights."
15. *Cottonwood Christian Center v. Cypress Redevelopment Agency*, United States District Court For The Central District of California, 218 F. Supp. 2d 1203; 2002.
16. James Bovard, "Zoning: The New Tyranny," *The Future of Freedom Foundation*, Aug. 1996 < http://www.fff.org/freedom/0896d.asp > (Accessed 29 July 2005).
17. Mark Brown, "Suburb Truck-Parking Ban Upheld," *Chicago Sun-Times*, June 27, 1996.
18. Bovard, "Zoning."
19. Ibid.
20. Peter Marks, "Unauthorized Use of Pumpkins Causes a Dispute; East Hampton Tells Jerry Della Femina to Follow Its Design Rules, and He Protests," *New York Times*, Dec. 1, 1993.
21. Bovard, "Zoning."
22. Chris Norby, "Don't Always Turn the Other Cheek, You Have Rights," in *Faith-Based not Bureaucracy-Bound*, ed. Ken Masugi (Claremont, CA: The Claremont Institute, 2004), 3.
23. *Kelo v. City of New London* 125. S. Ct. 2655; L Ed. 2d 439.
24. From the dissenting opinion in *Kelo v. The City of New London*, Cornell University, Legal Information Institute < http://straylight.law.cornell.edu/supct/html/04-108ZD.html > (Accessed 29 July 2005).
25. O'Connor, dissent, *Kelo*.
26. See, for example, Victor Davis Hanson, *The Western Way of War*, 32.
27. Robert D. Putnam, *Bowling Alone: The Collapse and Revival of American Community* (New York: Simon and Schuster, 2000).
28. See John Marini, *The Politics of Budget Control* (Washington, D.C.: Crane Russak, 1992).
29. See Edward J. Erler's discussion of Woodrow Wilson and the administrative state in *The American Polity* (New York: Crane Russak, 1991), 63. See also William L. Riordon, *Plunkitt of Tammany Hall*, intro. Peter Quinn (New York: Signet Classic, 1995); John Marini,

"Western Justice: John Ford and Sam Peckinpah on the Defense of the Heroic," in *The California Republic: Institutions, Statesmanship, and Policies*, eds. Brian P. Janiskee and Ken Masugi (Lanham, MD: Rowman & Littlefield, 2004): 265-278. In particular, note Marini's analysis of the classic Western film, *The Man Who Shot Liberty Valance*.

Appendix

Lexis/Nexis (U.S. News) Search Results, Resolutions, City Council, non-municipal, non-binding, March 1, 2003-March 1, 2005, by regional news sources, reverse chronological order.

Midwest

Scheer, Derek. "Now's the Time to Speak Out on Great Lakes." *Capital Times* (Madison, WI) 16 Oct. 2004: 11A.

"Joyo offers free showing of 'Unconstitutional.' " *Lincoln Journal Star* (NE) 24 Sept. 2004: 6.

"Dispute Brewing in Pine Bluff, Ark., over Reparations Resolution." *Associated Press State and Local Wire* 14 Aug. 2004.

"City Council Passes Resolution Opposing Patriot Act." *Associated Press State and Local Wire* 27 Jul. 2004.

Henrikson, Alicia. "Council Denounces White Supremacist Position." *Topeka Capital-Journal* (KN) 28 Apr. 2004.

"Ames Council Opposed Portions of Patriot Act." *Associated Press State and Local Wire* 25 Mar. 2004.

"Ann Arbor City Council Votes to Oppose Ban on Same-Sex Marriage." *Associated Press State and Local Wire* 16 Mar. 2004.

"Madison Council Passes Resolution Supporting Gay Marriage." *Associated Press State and Local Wire* 3 Mar. 2004.

"College Town's City Council Wants Revisions of USA Patriot Act." *Associated Press State and Local Wire* 4 Feb. 2004.

Pickett, Debra and Fran Spielman. "Council Urges Ashcroft to Investigate Till Case." *Chicago Sun-Times* 15 Jan. 2004: 8.

Neal, Steve. "Alderman Wants Japan to Pay for Crimes Against U.S. POWs." *Chicago-Sun Times* 5 Dec. 2003: 53.

Spielman, Fran. "Council Decries Patriot Act in Watered-Down Resolution." *Chicago Sun-Times* 2 Oct. 2003: 16.

"Ann Arbor City Council Passes Resolution on Patriot Act." *Associated Press State and Local Wire* 8 Jul. 2003.

Diaz, Kevin. "Anti-Terror Patriot Act Prompts Grass-Roots Uprising." *Star Tribune* (Minneapolis, MN) 23 May 2003: 19A.

"Council Right to Oppose Fee." *Capital Times* (Madison, WI) 8 May 2003: 16.

"Madison Council Passes Free-Speech Resolution." *Associated Press State and Local Wire* 9 Apr. 2003.

Northeast

LaFleur, Michael. "City Councilors Launch Missile vs. Patriot Act." *Lowell Sun* (Lowell, MA) 17 Nov. 2004.

"Not a 'Natural Person.'" *The Providence Journal* (Providence, RI) 6 Jul. 2004.

"Preserving Liberties; New Legislation in Congress Would Curb Patriot Act Excesses." *The Times Union* (Albany, NY): A10.

"Patterson Passes Anti-Patriot Act Resolutions." *Associated Press State and Local Wire* 10 Jun. 2004.

"Staying Safe and Free." *Pittsburgh Post-Gazette* 9 May 2004: B1.

"Vergennes Call on Residents to Display Yellow Ribbons." *Associated Press State and Local Wire* 6 Apr. 2004.

"Council to Consider Local Resolution about Patriot Act." *Portland Press Herald* (Maine) 13 Mar. 2004: 2B.

Andreatta, David. "Council Claims Federal Patriot Act Infringes on 'Fundamental Rights.'" *New York Times* 5 Feb. 2004: 3.

"Letters—Council's Wrong and Silly Patriot Vote." *Providence Journal-Bulletin* (RI) 21 Dec. 2003.

"Appalling 'No' Votes." *Pittsburgh Post-Gazette* 15 Dec. 2003: A18.

Mayerowitz, Scott. "Council Endorses Protest of Immigration Laws." *Providence Journal-Bulletin* (RI) 29 Sept. 2003.

Lombardi, Frank. "Council Anti-War Forces Win After Battle on Iraq." *Daily News* (New York, NY) 14 Mar. 2003: 1.

McLaughlin, Abraham. "In Minnesota, A Town of Veterans Divides over Iraq War." *Christian Science Monitor* 5 Mar 2003: 1.

Shontz, Lori. "Council Urges Diplomacy for Iraq." *Pittsburgh Post-Gazette* 5 Mar. 2003: B1.

Bouchard, Kelley. "Portland Plans Consolidation Cost-Cutting; The City Council Tells the Mayor to Form a Task Force to Find Ways to Share Costs with Neighbors." *Portland Press Herald* (ME) 4 Mar. 2003: B1.

Southeast

Yellig, John. "Charlottesville Faults Civil-Union Ban." *Richmond Times-Dispatch* (VA) 17 Nov. 2004: B4.

"2 Nights of Treats." *Chattanooga Times Free Pass* (TN) 17 Oct. 2004: B1.

Lively, Tarron. "Takoma Park Backs Gay Unions." *Washington Times* 15 Jul. 2004: B3.

"What's the Problem?" *News and Observer* (Raleigh, NC) 25 Jun. 2004.

Steffan, Kathy. "The Mandeville Backs Ban on Lake Dredging." *Times-Picayune* (New Orleans) 29 Apr. 2004: 1.

King, Lauren. "Elizabeth City Recognizes God's Role in U.S. History." *The Virginian Pilot* (Norfolk, VA) 23 Mar. 2004: Y1.

"With Bush in LA, Local Governments Oppose his Proposed Ban on Gay Marriage." *Associated Press State and Local Wire* 4 Mar. 2004.

"LA City Council Asks Congress to Throw Out Parts of Federal Patriot Act." *Associated Press State and Local Wire* 22 Jan. 2004.

"Kinston Council Approves Resolution Recognizing God." *Associated Press State and Local Wire* 21 Jan. 2004.

Aizenman, Nurith C. "Diversity Puts Vitality Into Aging Mt. Rainier; Community Reborn As Activist Enclave." *Washington Post* 30 Dec. 2003: B1.

Fowler, Bob. "Clinton Council Oks 'God Resolution.'" *Knoxville News-Sentinel* (TN) 17 Dec. 2003: B8.

Boyle, J.C. "Monument Supporters Are Models of Hypocrisy." *Atlanta Journal-Constitution* 18 Nov. 2003: 15A.

"Greene County Town Support Policy on Iraq." *Richmond Times Dispatch* (VA) 20 Mar. 2003.

Bell, Bret. "Savannah Takes Stand on Flag." *The Augusta Chronicle* (GA) 8 Mar. 2003: B5.

West

"News Briefs from California's Central Coast." *Associated Press State and Local Wire* 10 Feb. 2005.

"Council Backs Immigrant Aid." *Albuquerque Journal* (NM) 28 Jan. 2005: 4.

"Arcata; Impeachment of Bush, Cheney, Rumsfeld Urged." *Los Angeles Times* 9 Oct. 2004: 6.

Russo, Edward. "Eugene, Ore., Council Opposes Same-Sex Marriage Ban." *The Register Guard* 16 Sept. 2004.

"Aspen Leaders Oppose Same-Sex Marriage Ban." *Associated Press State and Local Wire* 14 Jul. 2004.

Richie, David. "Council Supports Gay-Marriage Ban." *Sacramento Bee* (CA) 17 Jun. 2004: G2.

"Aspen City Council Condemns Parts of Patriot Act." *Associated Press State and Local Wire* 15 Jun. 2004.

"Santa Cruz Officials Weigh in on Global Issues." *Associated Press State and Local Wire* 13 Jun. 2004.

Ammons, David. "Kerry, Bush Camps Spar Over Patriot Act." *Associated Press State and Local Wire* 3 Jun. 2004.

"Resolution Passed Honoring Those in the Armed Forces." *Wyoming Tribune Eagle* (Cheyenne, WY) 23 Mar. 2004: A4.

Hernandez, Barbara E. and Meghan Lewitt. "Palm Springs Joins Debate." *Press-Enterprise* (Riverside, CA) 19 Mar. 2004: B1.

MacDonald, Heather. "Oakland City Council Enters the Fray over Gay Marriage Resolution." *Alameda Times-Star* (Alameda, CA) 27 Feb. 2004.

Bee, Christine Vovakes. "Community to March Against Cross Burning." *Sacramento Bee* (CA) 8 Jan. 2004: B2.

"Group Urges Covers on Some Magazines." *Deseret News* (Salt Lake City, UT) 5 Jan. 2004: B2.

Wiener, Jocelyn. "It's a Day for Peace in Rocklin." *Sacramento Bee* (CA) 31 Dec. 2003: B2.

Stanton, Sam. "Patriot Act Under Fire." *Sacramento Bee* (CA) 15 Nov. 2003: B3.

"Community Snapshot." *The Oregonian* 31 Oct. 2003: D2.

Russell, Betsy Z. "Lawmaker to Take on Patriot Act." *Spokesman Review* (Spokane, WA) 24 Oct. 2003: B1.

"Bayard Joins Growing Anti-Patriot Act Movement." *Associated Press State and Local Wire* 23 Oct. 2003.

Steinberg, Scott. "Parts of Patriot Act Opposed." *Tri-Valley Herald* (Pleasanton, CA) 16 Oct. 2003.

"Austin City Council Opposes Patriot Act." *Associated Press State and Local Wire* 26 Sept. 2003.

Steinberg, Scott. "City Council Opposes Patriot Act." *Tri-Valley Herald* (Pleasanton, CA) 25 Sept. 2003.

"Albuquerque City Council Opposes Portions of Patriot Act." *Associated Press State and Local Wire* 16 Sept. 2003.

Eskenazi, Joe. "Berkeley Calls on U.S. to Probe Pro-Palestinian's Death." *Jewish Bulletin of Northern California* 12 Sept. 2003.

Mendoza, Martha. "Santa Cruz to Ask Congress to Consider Impeaching Bush." *Associated Press State and Local Wire* 10 Sept. 2003.

"Tiny Town Shouts 'Whoa!' to Patriot Act." *Associated Press State and Local Wire* 10 Aug. 2003.

Meyers, Michelle. "Hayward Objects to USA Patriot Act." *The Daily Review* (Hayward, CA) Jul. 24 2003.

"SoPas Chooses to Oppose Patriot Act." *Pasadena Star-News (Pasadena,* CA) 17 Jul. 2003.

"Lathrop Supports Area's Sikh Community; City Council Passes Resolution." *Tri-Valley Herald* (Pleasanton, CA) 23 Jun. 2003.

Martineau, Pamela. "Same-Sex Marriage Backed in Davis." *Sacramento Bee* (CA) 30 May 2003: B3.

"Philadelphia Panel Spurns Patriot Act." *San Diego Union Tribune* 30 May 2003: A7.

Lopez, Pablo. "Fresno Council Declares May Veterans Appreciation Month." *Fresno Bee* (CA) 14 May 2003: B4.

"LA City Council Urges Citizenship for Noncitizen Soldiers." *Associated Press State and Local Wire* 16 Apr. 2003.

"L.A. Council May Condemn Saddam." *The Daily News of Los Angeles* 11 Apr. 2003: N11.

"City Council Supports Troops, not Bush." *Associated Press State and Local Wire* 10 Apr. 2003.

"L.A. City Council Shows Support for Troops." *Associated Press State and Local Wire* 21 Mar. 2003.

Hernandez, Marjorie. "Camarillo Council Supports Troops in Gulf." *Ventura County Star* (CA) 10 Apr. 2003: B1.

Sherman, Lola. "Oceanside Voices Support for President, War in Iraq." *San Diego Union-Tribune* 9 Apr. 2003: NI-7.

Bova, Carl. "Mill Valley Opposes Patriot Act." *Marin Independent Journal* (CA) 8 Apr. 2003.

"Council Commends Bravery of Military." *San Diego Union-Tribune* 2 Apr. 2003: B2.

"City Supports Troops." *Spokesman Review* (Spokane, WA) 1 Apr. 2003: A7.

Cannata, Amy. "Airway Heights Supports U.S. Troops." *Spokesman Review* (Spokane, WA) 5 Mar. 2003: B4.

❋ ❋ ❋

BIBLIOGRAPHY

Adams, Charles Francis, Jr. *Three Episodes of Massachusetts History.* Boston: Houghton-Mifflin and Co., 1892.

Adams, Herbert Baxter. *The Germanic Origin of New England Towns.* Baltimore: Johns Hopkins University Press, 1882.

___. *Norman Constables in America.* Baltimore: Johns Hopkins University Press, 1883.

Adams, John. *Diary and Autobiography of John Adams*, vols. 1-3. Edited by L. H. Butterfield, Leonard C. Faber, and Wendell D. Garrett. Cambridge, MA: The Belknap Press of Harvard University Press, 1961.

___. *The Works of John Adams*, vols. 3, 4, 5, 7, 10. With a life of the author, notes, and illustrations by Charles Francis Adams. Boston: Little, Brown, and Company, 1856.

Adler, Moshe. "Ideology and the Structure of American and European Cities," *Journal of Urban History* 21, no. 6 (1995): 691-715.

Agrippa. "Letter II," and "Letter VII." In *The Complete Anti-Federalist,* vol. 4. Edited by Herbert J. Storing with the assistance of Murray Dry. Chicago: University of Chicago Press, 1981: 72-73, 81-83.

Allen, David Grayson. "The Zuckerman Thesis and the Process of Legal Rationalization in Provincial Massachusetts," *William and Mary Quarterly* 29, no. 3, 3rd Series (1972): 443-460.

___. *In English Ways: The Movement of Societies and the Transferal of English Local Law and Custom to Massachusetts Bay in the Seventeenth Century.* Chapel Hill, NC: University of North Carolina Press, 1981.

Andrews, Charles M. *The River Towns of Connecticut*. Baltimore: Johns Hopkins University Press, 1889.

Arendt, Hannah. *On Revolution*. New York: Viking Press, 1963.

Arensberg, Conrad M. "American Communities," *American Anthropologist* 57, no. 6 (1955): 1143-1162.

Axelrod, Donald. *Shadow Government: The Hidden World of Public Authorities—and How They Control over $1 Trillion of Your Money*. New York: John Wiley and Sons, 1992.

Baltzell, Edward Digby. *Puritan Boston and Quaker Philadelphia*. New York: The Free Press, 1979.

Becker, Carl. *The History of Political Parties in the Province of New York, 1760-1776*. Madison, WI: University of Wisconsin Press, 1909.

Beckman, Norman. "How Metropolitan are Federal and State Policies?" *Public Administration Review* 26 (1966): 96-106.

Berman v. Parker 348 U.S. 26; 75 S. Ct. 98; 99 L. Ed. 27; (1954).

Berrol, Selma Cantor. *The Empire City*. Westport, CT: Praeger, 1997.

Billings, Warren M., John E. Selby, and Thad W. Tate. *Colonial Virginia*. New York: KTO Press, 1986.

Bish, Robert L. *The Political Economy of Metropolitan Areas*. Chicago: Markham, 1971.

Blair, George S. *Government at the Grass-Roots*, 3rd ed. Pacific Palisades, CA: Palisades, 1981.

Bockelman, Wayne L. "Local Government in Colonial Pennsylvania." In *Town and County: Essays on the Structure of Local Government in the American Colonies*. Edited by Bruce C. Daniels. Middletown, CT: Wesleyan University Press, 1978: 216-237.

Bollens, John C. *Special District Government in the United States*. Berkeley: University of California Press, 1957.

Bollens, Scott A. "Examining the Link between State Policy and the Creation of Local Special Districts," *State and Local Government Review* 18 (1986): 117-124.

Bonomi, Patricia U. *A Factious People: Politics and Society in Colonial New York*. New York: Columbia University Press, 1971.

___. "Local Government in Colonial New York: A Base for Republicanism." In *Aspects of Early New York Society and Politics.* Edited by Jacob Judd and Irwin H. Polishook. Tarrytown, NY: Sleepy Hollow Restorations, 1974.

Bovard, James. "Zoning: The New Tyranny." The Future of Freedom Foundation, 1996. < http://www.fff.org/freedom/0896d.asp > (Accessed 29 July 2005).

Bradford, William. *History of Plymouth Plantation.* Boston: The Little, Brown, and Company, 1856.

Breen, Timothy H. "Persistent Localism: English Social Change and the Shaping of New England Institutions," *William and Mary Quarterly* 32, no. 1, 3rd Series (1975): 3-28.

___. "Who Governs: The Town Franchise in Seventeenth Century Massachusetts," *William and Mary Quarterly* 27, no. 3, 3rd Series (1970): 460-474.

Breen, Timothy H. and Stephen Foster. "The Puritans' Greatest Achievement: A Study of Social Cohesion in Seventeenth Century Massachusetts," *The Journal of American History* 60, no. 1 (1973): 5-22.

Bridenbaugh, Carl. *Cities in Revolt.* New York: Alfred A. Knopf, 1955.

___. *Cities in the Wilderness.* New York: The Ronald Press Co, 1938.

___. "The New England Town: A Way of Life," *American Antiquarian Society* 56 (1946): 19-48.

Brown, B. Katherine. "The Controversy over the Franchise in Puritan Massachusetts 1954-1974," *William and Mary Quarterly* 33, no. 2, 3rd Series (1976): 212-241.

Brown, Richard D. *Revolutionary Politics in Massachusetts.* Cambridge, MA: Harvard University Press, 1970.

___. "The Emergence of Urban Society in Rural Massachusetts, 1760-1820," *The Journal of American History* 61, no. 1 (1974): 29-51.

Brown, Richard D. and Jack Tager. *Massachusetts.* Amherst: University of Massachusetts Press, 2000.

Brown, Robert E. *Middle-Class Democracy and the Revolution in Massachusetts, 1691-1780.* Ithaca, NY: Cornell University Press, 1955.

Brugger, Robert J. *Maryland: A Middle Temperament, 1634-1980*. Baltimore: Johns Hopkins University Press, 1988.

Bryan, George. "The Genuine Principles of the Ancient Saxon, or English, Constitution." In *American Political Writing during the Founding Era*, vol. 1. Edited by Charles S. Hyneman and Donald S. Lutz. Indianapolis: Liberty Press, 1983: 340-367.

Burns, Nancy. *The Formation of American Local Governments*. New York: Oxford University Press, 1994.

Bushman, Richard L. *From Puritan to Yankee*. Cambridge, MA: Harvard University Press, 1969.

Callahan, Ellen Elizabeth. *Hadley: A Study of the Political Development of a Typical New England Town from the Official Records, 1659-1930*. Northampton, MA: Department of History, Smith College, 1931.

Carr, Lois Green. "The Foundation of Social Order: Local Government in Colonial Maryland." In *Town and County: Essays on the Structure of Local Government in the American Colonies*. Edited by Bruce C. Daniels. Middletown, CT: Wesleyan University Press, 1978: 72-110.

Channing, Edward. *Town and County Government in the English Colonies of North America*. Baltimore: Johns Hopkins University Press, 1884.

Chesterton, Gilbert Keith. *Orthodoxy*. Garden City, NY: Image Books, 1959.

Chudacoff, Howard. *The Evolution of American Urban Society*. Englewood Cliffs, NJ: Prentice-Hall, 1975.

Cohen, Charles T. "Mad Max (Weber) In New England," *Reviews in American History* 25, no. 1 (1997): 19-24.

Cook, Edward M., Jr. "Social Behavior and Changing Values in Dedham, MA, 1700 to 1775," *William and Mary Quarterly* 27, no. 4, 3rd Series (1970): 546-580.

Cooper, James F., Jr. "Higher Law, Free Consent, Limited Authority: Church Government and Political Culture in Seventeenth-Century Massachusetts," *New England Quarterly* 69, no. 2 (1996): 201-222.

Cottonwood Christian Center v. Cypress Redevelopment Agency. 218 F. Supp. 2d 1203 (2002).

Cox, Kevin R. and F. Z. Nartowicz, "Jurisdictional Fragmentation in the American Metropolis: Alternative Perspectives," *International Journal of Urban and Regional Research* 4 (1980): 196-211.

Dagger, Richard. "Metropolis, Memory, and Citizenship," *American Journal of Political Science* 25(1981): 715-737.

Daniels, Bruce C. *The Connecticut Town*. Middletown, CT: Wesleyan University Press, 1979.

___. "Connecticut Villages Become Mature Towns: The Complexity of Local Institutions," *William and Mary Quarterly* 34, no. 1, 3rd Series (1977): 83-103.

___. *Dissent and Conformity on Narragansett Bay*. Middletown, CT: Wesleyan University Press, 1983.

___. *The Fragmentation of New England*. New York: Greenwood Press, 1988.

___. "Introduction." In *Town and County: Essays on the Structure of Local Government in the American Colonies*. Edited by Bruce C. Daniels. Middletown, CT: Wesleyan University Press, 1978: 3-11.

___. "The Political Structure of Local Government in Colonial Connecticut." In *Town and County: Essays on the Structure of Local Government in the American Colonies*. Edited by Bruce C. Daniels. Middletown, CT: Wesleyan University Press, 1978: 44-71.

___, ed. *Town and County: Essays on the Structure of Local Government in the American Colonies*. Middletown, CT: Wesleyan University Press, 1978.

Danielson, Michael N. *Metropolitan Politics*, 2nd ed. Boston: Little Brown, 1965.

Danielson, Michael N. and Paul G. Lewis. "City Bound: Political Science and the American Metropolis," *Political Research Quarterly* 49, no. 1 (1996): 203-220.

Davis, W. T. *History of the Town of Plymouth*. New York: Charles Scribner and Sons, 1921.

Dennis, William C. "Kirk, Rossiter, Hartz, and the Conservative Tradition in America," *Modern Age* 24 (1980): 161-167.

Diamondstone, Judith. "The Government of Eighteenth Century

Philadelphia." In *Town and County: Essays on the Structure of Local Government in the American Colonies*. Edited by Bruce C. Daniels. Middletown, CT: Wesleyan University Press, 1978: 238-263.

Eddy, R. P. "In the End All Terrorism is Local." *The Times* (London). 8 July 2005: edition 3WC, 24.

Edgar, Walter. *South Carolina: A History*. Columbia, SC: University of South Carolina Press, 1998.

Egnal, Mark. *A Mighty Empire: The Origins of the American Revolution*. Ithaca: Cornell University Press, 1988.

Elazar, Daniel J. *Building Cities in America*. Lanham, MD: Hamilton Press, 1987.

Elkins, Stanley and Eric McKitrick. "A Meaning for Turner's Frontier: Part I: Democracy in the Old Northwest," *Political Science Quarterly* 69, no. 3 (1954): 321-353.

___. "A Meaning for Turner's Frontier: Part II: The Southwest Frontier and New England," *Political Science Quarterly* 69, no. 4 (1954): 565-602.

Ellis, David Maldwyn, James Frost, Harold C. Syrett, and Harry T. Carmen. *A History of New York State*. Ithaca: Cornell University Press, 1967.

Engeman, Thomas S. and Michael P. Zuckert, eds. *Protestantism and the American Founding*. Notre Dame, IN: University of Notre Dame Press, 2004.

Erler, Edward J. *The American Polity*. New York: Crane Russet, 1991.

Farnsworth-Milligan, Mary A. A. H. *Kith and Kin of the Georgia Ridge*. Newton, KS: United Print., 1973.

Franklin, Benjamin. *Benjamin Franklin's Autobiography*. Edited by J. A. Leo Lemay and P. M. Zall. New York: W. W. Norton and Company, 1986.

Fraser, Walter J. *Charleston! Charleston! The History of a Southern City*. Columbia, SC: University of South Carolina Press, 1989.

Friedersdorf, Conor. "Developer Wants to Build Next to Historic Winery." *Inland Valley Daily Bulletin* (Ontario, CA). 25 March 2005. *Lexis/Nexis* (Accessed 29 July 2005).

Fries, Sylvia Doughty. *The Urban Idea in Colonial America*. Philadelphia: Temple University Press, 1977.

Fund, John. "Property Rights are Civil Rights," Opinion Journal (*Wall Street Journal*), July 11, 2005 < http://www.opinionjournal.com/diary/?id = 110006941 > (Accessed 29 July 2005).

Gere, Edwin A., Jr. "Dillon's Rule and the Cooley Doctrine: Reflections of the Political Culture," *Journal of Urban History* 8, no. 3 (1982): 271-298.

German, James D. "The Social Utility of Wicked Self-Love: Calvinism, Capitalism, and Public Policy in Revolutionary New England," *The Journal of American History* 82, no. 3 (1995): 965-998.

Glaab, Charles N. and A. Theodore Brown. *A History of Urban America*. London: The Macmillan Co., 1972.

Glendenning, Parris N. and Mavis Mann Reeves. *Pragmatic Federalism: An Intergovernmental View of American Government*. Pacific Palisades, CA: Palisades, 1984.

Goodnow, Frank J. *Municipal Problems*. London: Macmillan Company, 1902.

Greenhut, Steven (*Orange County Register*), "Property Rights Not Just a Defense for the Rich." *Tulsa World* (Oklahoma), 15 August 2004, G4.

Griffith, Ernest S. and Charles R. Adrian. *A History of American City Government: The Formation of Traditions, 1775-1870*. Washington, DC: University Press of America, 1983.

Hall, Harold C. "Pierre Chastain: Controversy in Manakin Town." Paper presented at the annual meeting of the Pierre Chastain Family Association, Richmond, VA: October 2000.

Haller, William, Jr. *The Puritan Frontier: Town-Planting in New England Colonial Development, 1630-1660*. New York: Columbia University Press, 1951.

Hamilton, Alexander, James Madison, and John Jay. *The Federalist Papers*. Edited by Clinton Rossiter, with an introduction and notes by Charles Kesler. New York: Mentor, 1999.

Hanson, Victor Davis. *Carnage and Culture*. New York: Doubleday, 2001.

___. *The Soul of Battle*. New York: Free Press, 1999.

___. *The Western Way of War*. New York: Alfred A. Knopf, 1989.

Hardy, Beatriz Betancourt. "A Papist in a Protestant Age: The Case of Richard Bennett, 1667-1749," *Journal of Southern History* 60, no. 2 (1994): 203-228.

Harrigan, John J. *Political Change in the Metropolis*, 2nd ed. Boston: Little, Brown and Company, 1981.

Harvey, David. *Social Justice and the City*. Baltimore: Johns Hopkins University Press, 1973.

Hawkins, Robert B., Jr. *Self Government by District: Myth and Reality*. Stanford, CA: Hoover Institution Press, 1976.

Heiman, Michael Kenneth. *The Quiet Evolution*. New York: Praeger, 1989.

Henretta, James A. "The Morphology of New England Society in the Colonial Period," *Journal of Interdisciplinary History* 2 (1971): 379-399.

Henry, Patrick. "Speeches of Patrick Henry in the Virginia Ratifying Convention." In *The Complete Anti-Federalist*, vol. 5. Edited by Herbert J. Storing with assistance by Murray Dry. Chicago: University of Chicago Press, 1981: 207-254.

Higham, John. "Herbert Baxter Adams and the Study of Local History," *The American Historical Review* 89, no. 5 (1984): 1225-1239.

Jaffa, Harry V. *The Conditions of Freedom*. Baltimore: Johns Hopkins University Press, 1975.

___. *Crisis of the House Divided*. Chicago: University of Chicago Press, 1982.

___. *A New Birth of Freedom*. Lanham, MD: Rowman & Littlefield, 2000.

Jefferson, Thomas. *Notes on the State of Virginia*. Introduction and notes by William Peden. Chapel Hill: University of North Carolina Press, 1955.

___. *Papers of Thomas Jefferson*, vol. 1. Edited by Julian P. Boyd and Lyman H. Butterfield. Princeton, NJ: Princeton University Press, 1950.

___. *The Writings of Thomas Jefferson*, vols. 10, 12-16. Edited by Albert Ellery Bergh. Washington, DC: The Thomas Jefferson Memorial Association, 1907.

Jodziewicz, Thomas W. "'Vox Populi' Fairfield and Early Connecticut's Dual Localism," *New England Quarterly* 58 (1985): 578-607.

Johnston, Alexander. *Connecticut: A Study of a Commonwealth Democracy*. Boston: Houghton-Mifflin, 1890.

Judd, Jacob and Irwin H. Polishook, eds. *Aspects of Early New York Society and Politics*. Tarrytown, NY: Sleepy Hollow Restorations, 1974.

Kammen, Michael. *Colonial New York*. New York: Charles Scribner and Sons, 1975.

Kelo v. The City of New London. Cornell University, Legal Information Institute. < http://straylight.law.cornell.edu/supct/html/04-108ZO.html > (Accessed 29 July 2005).

Klebanow, Diana, Franklin L. Jonas, and Ira M. Leonard. *Urban Legacy*. New York: Mentor, 1977.

Konig, David Thomas. "English Legal Change and the Origins of Local Government in Northern Massachusetts." In *Town and County: Essays on the Structure of Local Government in the American Colonies*. Edited by Bruce C. Daniels. Middletown, CT: Wesleyan University Press, 1978: 12-43.

Kotkin, Joel. "City Of the Future: Unless it keeps its citizens safe, the modern metropolis may go the way of ancient Rome." *Washington Post*. July 24, 2005: B 1.

Labaree, Benjamin W. *Colonial Massachusetts: A History*. Millwood, NY: KTO Press, 1979.

Land, Aubrey C. *Colonial Maryland: A History*. Millwood, NY: KTO Press, 1981.

Lefler, Hugh T., and William S. Powell. *Colonial North Carolina*. New York: Charles Scribner and Sons, 1973.

Lévi-Strauss, Claude. *Structural Anthropology*. New York: Basic Books, 1963.

Lincoln, Abraham. *The Collected Works of Abraham Lincoln*, vol. 8. New Brunswick, NJ: Rutgers University Press, 1953.

Lingeman, Richard. *Small Town America: A Narrative History: 1620 to the Present*. New York: G.P. Putnam and Sons, 1980.

Little Hoover Commission. *Special Districts: Relics of the Past or Resources for the Future*. Sacramento: State of California, 2000.

Locke, John. *Second Treatise on Government*. Arlington Heights, IL: Harlan Davidson, 1982.

Lockridge, Kenneth A. *A New England Town: The First Hundred Years*. New York: W.W. Norton and Co, 1985.

Lockridge, Kenneth A. and Alan Kreider. "The Evolution of Massachusetts Town Government, 1640 to 1740," *William and Mary Quarterly* 23, no. 4, 3rd Series (1966): 549-557.

Machor, James L. *Pastoral Cities: Urban Ideals and the Symbolic Landscape of America*. Madison, WI: University of Wisconsin Press, 1987.

Maclear, Anne Bush. *Early New England Towns. A Comparative Study of Their Development*. New York: AMS Press, 1967.

MacManus, Susan A. "Special District Governments: A Note on Their Use as Property Tax Relief Mechanisms in the 1970s," *Journal of Politics* 43 (1981): 1207-1214.

Madison, James. *Letters and Other Writings of James Madison*, vol. 1. New York: R. Worthington, 1884.

___. *The Papers of James Madison*, vol. 8. Edited by Robert A. Rutland, William M. E. Rachal, Barbara D. Ripel, and Fredrika J. Teute. Chicago: University of Chicago Press, 1973.

Marini, John. *The Politics of Budget Control*. Washington, D.C: Crane Russak, 1992.

___. "Western Justice: John Ford and Sam Peckinpah on the Defense of the Heroic." In *The California Republic: Institutions, Statesmanship, and Policies*. Edited by Brian P. Janiskee and Ken Masugi. Lanham, MD: Rowman & Littlefield, 2004: 265-278.

Martin, Harold H. *Georgia*. New York: W.W. Norton and Company, 1977.

Marx, Leo. *The Machine in the Garden*. New York: Oxford University Press, 1967.

Matthews, Richard. *The Radical Politics of Thomas Jefferson*. Lawrence, KS: University of Kansas Press, 1984.

Maxey, Chester. "The Political Integration of Metropolitan Communities," *National Municipal Review* 11(1922): 229-252.

McCullough, David. *John Adams*. New York: Simon and Schuster, 2001.

McGiffert, Michael. "American Puritan Studies in the 1960s," *William and Mary Quarterly* 27, no. 1, 3rd Series (1970): 36-67.

McKelvey, Blake. *The City in American History*. London: Allen and Unwin, 1969.

McKinley, Albert E. "The English and Dutch Towns of New Netherland," *The American Historical Review* 6, no. 1 (1900): 1-18.

McLoughlin, William G. *Rhode Island*. New York: W.W. Norton, 1978.

Merwick, Donna. "Dutch Townsmen and Land Use: A Spatial Perspective on Seventeenth-Century Albany, New York," *William and Mary Quarterly* 37, no. 1, 3rd Series (1980): 53-78.

Miller, Joshua. "Direct Democracy and the Puritan Theory of Membership," *The Journal of Politics* 53, no. 1 (1991): 57-74.

Miller, Perry. *The New England Mind: From Colony to Province*. Cambridge, MA: Harvard University Press, 1962.

___. *The New England Mind: The Seventeenth Century*. Cambridge, MA: Harvard University Press, 1963.

Monkkonen, Eric H. *America Becomes Urban*. Berkeley, CA: The University of California Press, 1988.

Montesquieu, Charles de Secondat, Baron de. *The Spirit of the Laws*. New York: Cambridge University Press, 1989.

Morgan, Edmund S. *American Slavery, America Freedom: The Ordeal of Colonial Virginia*. New York: W.W. Norton and Company, Inc., 1975.

Mumford, Lewis. *The City in History*. New York: Harcourt, Brace, and World Inc., 1961.

Munroe, John A. *Colonial Delaware*. New York: KTO Press, 1978.

Nash, Gary B. *First City: Philadelphia and the Forging of Historical Memory*. Philadelphia: University of Pennsylvania Press, 2002.

___. *The Urban Crucible*. Cambridge, MA: Harvard University Press, 1979.

Nash, R. C. "Urbanization in the Colonial South: Charleston, South Carolina as a Case Study," *Journal of Urban History* 9, no. 1 (1992): 3-29.

National Municipal League, Committee on Metropolitan Government. *The Government of Metropolitan Areas*. New York: Author, 1930.

Nelson, Michael A. "Decentralization of the Subnational Public Sector: An Empirical Analysis of the Determinants of Local Government Structure in Metropolitan Areas in the US," *Southern Economic Journal* 57 (1990): 443-457.

Nevins, Allan. *The American States During and After the Revolution, 1778-1789*. New York: Macmillan Co., 1927.

Norby, Chris. "Don't Always Turn the Other Cheek, You Have Rights." In *Faith-Based not Bureaucracy-Bound*. Edited by Ken Masugi. Claremont, CA: The Claremont Institute, 2004: 1-8.

O'Connor, Thomas H. *Bibles, Brahmins, and Bosses*, 2nd ed., revised. Boston: Trustees of the Public Library of the City of Boston, 1984.

Osgood, Herbert L. *The American Colonies in the Seventeenth Century*, 4 vols. New York: Columbia University Press, 1958.

Ostrom, Elinor. "The Danger of Self-Evident Truths," *PS: Political Science and Politics* 23 (2000): 33-44.

Ostrom, Vincent. *The Meaning of American Federalism*. San Francisco, ICS Press, 1991.

___. "Where to Begin?" *Publius* 25 (1995): 45-60.

Ostrom, Vincent, Robert Bish, and Elinor Ostrom. *Local Government in the United States*. San Francisco: Institute for Contemporary Studies Press, 1988.

Ostrom, Vincent, Charles Tiebout, and Robert Warren. "The Organization of Government in Metropolitan Areas: A Theoretical Inquiry," *American Political Science Review* 55 (1961): 831-842.

Pangle, Thomas L. *The Spirit of Modern Republicanism*. Chicago: University of Chicago Press, 1988.

Pestana, Carla Gardina. "The Quaker Executions as Myth and History," *The Journal of American History* 80 (1993): 441-469.

Peterson, Paul. *City Limits*. Chicago: University of Chicago Press, 1981.

Pole, J. R. *Paths to the American Past*. New York: Oxford University Press, 1979.

Poletown Neighborhood Council v. Detroit 410 Mich. 616, 304 N.W. 2d 455 (1981).

Pomfret, John E. *Colonial New Jersey: A History.* New York: Charles Scribner's Sons, 1973.

Powell, Sumner Chilton. *Puritan Village: The Formation of a New England Town.* Middletown, CT: Wesleyan University Press, 1963.

Powell, William S. *North Carolina.* New York: W.W. Norton and Co., 1977.

Putnam, Robert D. *Bowling Alone: The Collapse and Revival of American Community.* New York: Simon and Schuster, 2000.

Quinn, Christopher. "Shopowners Cry Foul: Stockbridge Couple Says City Blocked Sale to Seize Property." *Journal-Constitution* (Atlanta, GA), 4 July 2005, E1.

Reed, Thomas H. "The Government of Metropolitan Areas," *Public Management* 12 (1930): 75-78.

Reed, Thomas H. "Progress in Metropolitan Integration," *Public Administration Review* 9 (1949): 1-10.

Riordon, William L. *Plunkitt of Tammany Hall.* With a new introduction by Peter Quinn. New York: Signet Classic, 1995.

Rodgers, Daniel T. "Republicanism: The Career of a Concept," *Journal of American History* 79, no. 1 (1992): 11-38.

Roper, Louis H. "The Unraveling of an Anglo-America Utopia in South Carolina," *The Historian* 58 (1996): 277-288.

Rubin, Louis D., Jr. *Virginia.* New York: W.W. Norton and Company, 1977.

Rusk, David. *Cities Without Suburbs.* Washington, DC: Woodrow Wilson Center Press, 1993.

Rutman, Darrett B. *Winthrop's Boston: Portrait of a Puritan Town, 1630-1649.* Chapel Hill, NC: University of North Carolina Press, 1965.

Schudson, Michael. *The Good Citizen: A History of American Civic Life.* Cambridge, MA: Harvard University Press, 1991.

Scott, Stanley and John Corzine. "Special Districts in the San Francisco Bay Area." In *Metropolitan Politics*, 2nd ed. Edited by Michael N. Danielson. Boston: Little Brown, 1966: 246-260.

Seiler, William H. "The Anglican Church: A Basic Institution of Local Government in Colonial Virginia." In *Town and County: Essays on the Structure of Local Government in the American Colonies*. Edited by Bruce C. Daniels. Middletown, CT: Wesleyan University Press, 1978: 134-159.

Sennett, Richard. "American Cities: The Grid Plan and the Protestant Ethic," *International Social Science Journal* 42, no. 3 (1990): 269-285.

Seybolt, Robert Francis. *The Colonial Citizen of New York City*. Madison, WI: University of Wisconsin Press, 1918.

Shain, Barry Alan. "The Americanization of Conservatism," *Modern Age* 42, no. 1 (2000): 118-127.

Shalhope, Robert E. *John Taylor of Caroline: Pastoral Republican*. Columbia, SC: University of South Carolina Press, 1980.

___. *The Roots of Democracy*. Boston: Twayne Publishers, 1990.

Shepard, Odell. *Connecticut: Past and Present*. New York: Alfred A. Knopf, 1890.

Sirmans, M. Eugene. *Colonial South Carolina*. Chapel Hill: University of North Carolina Press, 1966.

Sly, John Farifield. *Town Government in Massachusetts, 1620-1930*. Hamden, CT: Archon Books, 1967.

Small, Judy Jo. "Robert Beverley and the New World Garden," *American Literature* 55, no.4 (1983): 525-40.

Smith, David A. "Dependent Urbanization in Colonial America: The Case of Charleston, SC," *Social Forces* 66, no. 1 (1987): 1-28.

Smith, Donald T. "Rethinking the Colonial Generalities: Putting the Cod and Cohesion in Their Places," *The History Teacher* 26, no. 2 (1993): 233-245.

Smith, Page P. *As a City Upon a Hill*. Cambridge, MA: MIT, 1973.

Smith, Robert G. "Special Purpose Governments," *The American County* 36 (1971): 10-17.

Smolinski, Reiner. "Israel Redivivus: The Eschatological Limits of Puritan Theology in New England," *The New England Quarterly* 63, no. 3 (1990): 357-395.

Steiner, Bruce E. "Anglican Office-Holding in Pre-Revolutionary Connecticut: The Parameters of New England Community,"

William and Mary Quarterly 31, no. 3, 3rd Series (1974): 369-406.

Stephens, G. Ross and Nelson Wikstrom. "Trends in Special Districts," *State and Local Government Review* 30 (1998): 129-138.

Stephenson, Bruce. "The Roots of the New Urbanism: John Nolen's Garden City Ethic," *Journal of Planning History* 1, no. 2 (2002): 99-123.

Syrett, David. "Town Meeting Politics in Massachusetts: 1776-1786," *William and Mary Quarterly* 21, no. 3, 3rd Series (1964): 352-366.

Tacitus, Cornelius. *Agricola and Germany*. Translated with an introduction and notes by Anthony R. Birley. New York: Oxford University Press, 1999.

Taylor, Robert J. *Colonial Connecticut: A History*. Millwood, NY: KTO Press, 1979.

Teaford, Jon C. *The Municipal Revolution in America*. Chicago: The University of Chicago Press, 1975.

Tefler, Hugh T., William S. Powell. *Colonial North Carolina*. New York: Charles Scribner and Sons, 1973.

Teske, Paul, Mark Schneider, Michael Mintrom, and Samuel Best. "Establishing the Micro Foundations of Macro Theory: Information, Movers, and the Competitive Local Market for Public Goods," *American Political Science Review* 87 (1993): 702-713.

Thompson, Roger. "Enough of Thorough: Watertown as a Case of Early Massachusetts Town Government," *The New England Quarterly* 73, no. 4 (2000): 560-582.

Thorpe, Francis Newton, ed. *The Federal and State Constitutions, Colonial Charters, and Other Organic Laws of the States, Territories, and Colonies*, 7 vols. Washington, DC: Government Printing Office, 1909.

Tiebout, Charles M. "A Pure Theory of Local Expenditures," *Journal of Political Economy* 64 (1956): 416-424.

Tinkcom, Harry Marlin. *The Republicans and Federalists in Pennsylvania, 1790-1801*. Harrisburg, PA: Pennsylvania Historical and Museum Commission, 1950.

Tobler, Waldo. "Geographic Area and Map Projection," *Geographical Review* 53 (1963): 59-78.

Tocqueville, Alexis De. *Democracy in America*. Edited, translated, and with an introduction by Harvey C. Mansfield and Delba Winthrop. Chicago: University of Chicago Press, 2000.

Trewartha, Glenn T. "Types of Rural Settlement in Colonial America," *Geographical Review* 36, no. 4 (1946): 568-596.

Turner, Frederick Jackson. *History, Frontier, and Section: Three Essays*. University of New Mexico Press, 1993.

Varga, Nicholas. "The Development and Structure of Local Government in Colonial New York." In *Town and County: Essays on the Structure of Local Government in the American Colonies*. Edited by Bruce C. Daniels. Middletown, CT: Wesleyan University Press, 1978: 186-215.

Viteritti, Joseph P. and Gerald Russello. "Community and American Federalism: Images Romantic and Real," *Virginia Journal of Social Policy and the Law* 4 (1997): 683-742.

Wallace, Mike and Edwin G. Burrows. *Gotham: A History of New York City to 1898*. New York: Oxford University Press, 1999.

Warden, G. B. "The Caucus and Democracy in Colonial Boston," *The New England Quarterly* 43, no. 1(1970): 19-45.

Warner, Sam Bass, Jr. *The Private City: Philadelphia in Three Periods of Its Growth*. Philadelphia: University of Pennsylvania Press, 1987.

___. *The Urban Wilderness*. New York: Harper and Row Publishers, 1972.

Warren, Robert B. "A Municipal Services Market Model for Metropolitan Organization," *Journal of the American Institute Planners* 30 (1964): 193-204.

Washington, George. *The Writings of George Washington*, vol. 34. Edited by John C. Fitzpatrick. Washington, DC: United States Government Printing Office, 1931.

Waterhouse, Richard. "The Responsible Gentry of Colonial South Carolina: A Study in Local Government." In *Town and County: Essays on the Structure of Local Government in the American Colonies*. Edited by Bruce C. Daniels, Middletown, CT: Wesleyan University Press, 1978: 160-185.

Weir, Robert M. *Colonial South Carolina: A History.* Millwood, NY: KTO Press, 1983.

West, Thomas G. "The Transformation of Protestant Theology as a Condition of the American Revolution." In *Protestantism and the American Founding.* Edited by Thomas S. Engeman and Michael P. Zuckert. Notre Dame, IN: University of Notre Dame Press, 2004: 187-224.

___. *Vindicating the Founders.* Lanham, MD: Rowman & Littlefield, 1997.

Westbrook, Perry D. *The New England Town in Fact and Fiction.* Rutherford, NJ: Farleigh Dickinson University Press, 1982.

Wheeler, Robert. "The County Court in Colonial Virginia." In *Town and County: Essays on the Structure of Local Government in the American Colonies.* Edited by Bruce C. Daniels. Middletown, CT: Wesleyan University Press, 1978: 111-133.

Willingham, William F. "Deference Democracy and Town Government in Windham, Connecticut, 1755-1786," *William and Mary Quarterly* 30, 3rd Series (1973): 401-422.

Wilson, James. *The Works of James Wilson,* 2 vols. Edited by Robert Green McCloskey. Cambridge, MA: The Belknap Press of the Harvard University Press, 1967.

Winson, Gail I. "Researching the Laws of the Colony of Rhode Island and Providence Plantations," Roger Williams University School of Law Faculty Papers, no. 1 (2003): 1-39. < http://lsr.nellco.org/cgi/viewcontent.cgi?article = 1000&context = rwu/rwufp > (Accessed 19 January 2005.)

Winter, William O. *State and Local Government in a Decentralized Republic.* New York: Macmillan Publishing Co., 1981.

___. *The Urban Polity.* Toronto: The University of Toronto, 1969.

Wood, Gordon S. "A Century of Writing Early American History," *The American Historical Review* 100, no. 3 (1995): 678-696.

Wood, Joseph S. "Build Therefore Your Own World: The New England Village as Settlement Ideal," *Annals of the Association of American Geographers* 81, no. 1 (1991): 32-50.

___. *The New England Village.* With a Contribution by Michael P. Steinitz. Baltimore: Johns Hopkins University, 1997.

___. "Village and Community in Early Colonial New England,"

Journal of Historical Geography 8, no. 4 (1982): 333-346.

Wright, Louis B. *South Carolina.* New York: W.W. Norton, 1976.

Yarbrough, Jean M. *American Virtues: Thomas Jefferson on the Character of a Free People.* Lawrence, KS: University of Kansas Press, 1998.

Zuckerman, Michael. "Michael Zuckerman's Reply," *William and Mary Quarterly* 29, no. 3, 3rd Series (1972): 461-468.

___. *Peaceable Kingdoms: New England Towns in the Eighteenth Century.* New York: Alfred A Knopf, 1970.

___. "The Social Context of Democracy in Massachusetts," *William and Mary Quarterly* 25, no. 1, 3rd Series (1968): 523-544.

Zuckert, Michael P. "Natural Rights and Protestant Politics." In *Protestantism and the American Founding.* Edited by Thomas S. Engeman and Michael P. Zuckert. Notre Dame, IN: University of Notre Dame Press, 2004: 21-76.

___. *The Natural Rights Republic.* Notre Dame, IN: The University of Notre Dame Press, 1996.

✹ ✹ ✹

About the Author

Brian Janiskee received his Ph.D. from Michigan State University and is professor and Chair of the Department of Political Science at California State University, San Bernardino, where he is also a faculty member in the national security studies program. In addition, he is a research fellow at the Claremont Institute. He is the co-author of *Democracy in California: Politics and Government in the Golden State* (Rowman & Littlefield, 2008). This text uses many ideas raised by Tocqueville to analyze the current workings of California politics. In addition, Janiskee has coedited a collection of essays on California politics titled *The California Republic: Institutions, Statesmanship, and Policies* (Rowman & Littlefield, 2004). He has also published several scholarly articles on topics ranging from crime policy to presidential elections to special district local governments.

About the Claremont Institute

The Claremont Institute for the Study of Statesmanship and Political Philosophy was founded in 1979 to restore the principles of the American Founding to their rightful, preeminent authority in our national life. The Institute publishes the quarterly Claremont Review of Books, sponsors serveral educational fellowships in the American Founding and conducts a variety of programs that apply the principles of the Founding to the critical public policy issues of our day. Our scholarship extends from strategic to literary studies, from Plato and Aristotle to John Locke and Thomas Jefferson—in short, to all those subjects upon which citizens must draw to preserve and perfect their liberty.

The Claremont Institute
937 West Foothill Blvd.
Claremont, Ca 91711
909-621-6825

INDEX

Adams, Charles Francis, Jr., 5, 10, 21, 24, 26, 41-42, 90, 95, 103, 120-123
Adams, Herbert Baxter, 5, 10, 90, 128
Adams, John, 2, 5, 9, 13, 24, 39, 74, 83-84, 86-87, 92-95, 101, 112, 120-123, 125, 143
administrative state, xi, 131, 140, 143-144, 149
Adrian, Charles R., 10
Alfred the Great, 85
American Indian, 4, 128
American Revolution, 3, 9, 13, 50, 93, 101, 106, 109, 115-116, 131, 134, 141
Andrews, Charles, 31, 39, 43-44, 122
Anti-Federalists, 6, 8, 84, 107, 128
Antinomian Crisis, 18-19
Anti-Quaker, 51
Arendt, Hannah, 111, 113-114, 116
Arensberg, Conrad M., 10
autocratic rule, 47, 83
autonomy, 17, 59, 61, 117-118, 125, 133

Bacon's Rebellion, 51, 75
Baker v. Carr, 134, 150
Bank of England, 71
Battle of Golden Hill, 56, 77
Becker, Carl, 75
Berkeley, John, 57
Berman v. Parker, 135-136, 150
Berrol, Selma Cantor, 76-77
Billings, Warren M., 79-80
Bockelman, Wayne, 59, 78
Bonomi, Patricia, 53, 75-76

Boston, MA, 3, 24, 28, 40, 48, 55, 56, 104, 122, 138
Boston Massacre, 56
Bovard, James, 137-138, 151
Bradford, William, 43, 90
Braintree, MA, 21, 26-28, 91, 95-97
Bridenbaugh, Carl, 10, 19, 23-24, 35, 40-42, 44-45, 75-77, 80, 122
British currency, 25, 42
Brown, John, 108
Brown, B. Katherine, 40
Brown, Mark, 151
Brown, Richard D., 41
Brown, Robert D., 24, 41, 97
Brown, Robert E., 20, 39, 41-43
Brown, Theodore A., 81
Bryan, George, 6, 128-129
Burrows, Edwin, 56, 75-77
Bushman, Richard, 32, 43-44

Callahan, Ellen, 20, 39-41, 122
Calverts, 51, 61-62
Calvinism, 116
Calvinist Protestantism, 7, 18
Cambridge, MA, 19, 97
capital sentence, 17, 65
Carol Stream, IL, 137
Carr, Lois Green, 78-79
Cartwright, John, 112, 129
Cateret, George, 57
Cato, 115
Channing, Edward, 39, 41-42, 79-80
Charles II, 34, 75
Charleston, SC, 3, 50-51, 54, 69-70
Charter of 1663, 16

181

Charter of 1691, 15, 18, 27
Charter of Delaware, 61
Chudacoff, Howard, 75
Church of England, 64, 69
clerk, 21-23, 26-27, 35, 38, 60-61, 63, 66-67
colonial assembly, 16, 66
commissioner, 22-23, 26, 58, 60, 73
Concession and Agreement of 1664, 57-58
Connecticut: Calvinists, 31; Charter, 30; county court, 33; court of assistants, 34; "deference democracy," 31; *Fundamental Orders*, 16, 30; General Court, 30; Puritans, 31
constable, 17, 20, 22-24, 26, 29, 35, 38, 44, 52-53, 55, 60-61, 63, 66-67, 71-72, 87, 106
Coral Gables, FL, 137
corporal punishment, 17, 99
Cottonwood Christian Center, 136, 151
County of Wayne v. Hatchcock, 151
courts, 74, 85, 104
Crown, the, 4, 22, 29-30, 56, 58, 62, 68, 70-71, 74, 83-84, 87, 103, 104

Daniels, Bruce, 30, 33-37, 39-40, 42-45, 75, 78-80, 122
David, W. T., 121
decentralized, ix, 14-16, 38, 47, 84, 125
Declaration of Independence, ix, 100, 148
Dedham, MA, 19, 22
Defence of the Constitutions of Government of the United States of America, 13, 105
Delaware: Anglo-Saxon tradition, 62; Lower Counties, 62; structure of local government, 61
Democracy in America, 1, 99, 114
Demophilus, 128
deputies, 15-19, 35, 57, 72, 85-87
Diamondstone, Judith, 75
Dorchester, MA, 19, 97
drink, 72, 94, 105, 115-116, 143

Duke's Release, 57

East India Company, 49
East Jersey, 57
Eddy, R. P., 150
Edgar, Walter, 80
education, 27-28, 42
Egbert, 85
Elkins, Stanley, 11
Embargo Act, 115, 133
Emerson, Ralph Waldo, 90
eminent domain, 135-136, 138-140
Erler, Edward J., 151
excise taxes, 38, 57, 60
executions, 8, 53
export duties, 38, 68, 73

Federalist, The, 2, 100, 130
Federalists, 6, 85, 128
fence-viewer, 22-23, 35, 38, 53-54
fines, 17, 20-21, 24, 32, 37, 64, 87, 97-98, 126
Founders on Local Government, 83-119
Founders, the, ix, 2-3, 9, 13-14, 30, 71, 99, 118, 126-132, 140-141, 143, 149
Franklin, Benjamin, 84, 87, 120
Fraser, Walter J., 80
freemen, 17-18, 40, 52, 54, 59-60, 69, 76
Fries, Sylvia Doughty, 75, 78-79, 81
frontier, 4, 6-7, 13-14, 49-50, 65, 70, 72
Fund, John, 151
Fundamental Orders of 1639, 16, 30

General Motors, 135-136
George III, 38
Georgia: Board of Trustees, 70-71; *Charter of Georgia*, 70; green town, 72; prohibition, 72; settlers, 72
German, 5-6, 49
Giuliani, Rudy, 141
Glaab, Charles N., 81
Glendenning, Parris, 11, 117, 124
government autonomy, 133
Governor Andros, 49
Governor Sloughter, 53

INDEX

governors, 49, 84, 87, 109, 111, 128
Grayson, David, 121
Greek phalanx, 116, 141
Greenhut, Steven, 150-151
Griffith, Ernest S., 10

Hadley, MA, 20-21
Hall, Harold, 64, 79, 81
Hamilton, Alexander, 11, 130
Hanson, Victor Davis, 123, 151
Henry, Patrick, 84, 107-109, 119, 123
heresy, 8, 99
hiving-off, 33
Huguenot, 64-65
hundreds, 62, 111, 113
Hussein, Saddam, 146, 148
Hutchinson, Anne, 34

import duties, 38
independence, 62, 104, 110
inhabitants, 17-19, 28, 40, 52, 56, 63, 106-107, 110
Iraq War, 144, 146

James II, 38, 52
Jefferson, Thomas, xii, 2-3, 9, 50, 74, 83-84, 86-89, 92-93, 101-102, 111-121, 123-126, 129-131, 133-134, 141, 143-144, 150
Judd, Jacob, 76
jury, 27, 35, 63, 79

Kammen, Michael, 75
Kelo v. New London, 138-140, 150-151
Kentucky, 108
Kercheval, Samuel, 114
King George II, 70
King George's War, 72
King Phillip's War, 16
King William's War, 71
Klebanow, Diana, 10
Konig, David Thomas, 42
Kotkin, Joel, 150

Labaree, Benjamin Woods, 39-40
land allocation, 32
Lee, Richard Henry, 86
Leisler Revolt, 49
Leisler, Jacob, 49, 53

Lewis, Robert, 85
local autonomy, 117-118
local democracy, 6
local government: centralized, 13, 14, 48-50, 73, 83-84, 119; structure, 5, 13, 15, 17, 38, 48, 51, 61, 73, 126; virtue, 111, 133
local politics: contact, 126; gateway, 119, 126, 150
Lockridge, Kenneth, 19, 39-41
London, 4, 6, 72
Los Angeles, CA, 137, 145-146

Mably, Abbé de, 39, 106
Maclear, Anne Bush, 19, 27, 39-42, 97, 122
Madison, James, x, 2, 8-9, 11, 84-86, 98, 100-101, 107-109, 120, 123, 134-135
Marini, John, 151
Marks, Peter, 151
Martin, Harold H., 81
Maryland: county coroner, 62; county sheriff, 62; Revolution of 1689, 62, 64; taxes, 63
Massachusetts: court of assistants, 27; courts, 26-27
Massachusetts and Plymouth Colonies, 29
Massachusetts Bay Colony, 14, 29, 32
Masugi, Ken, xii, xiv
Matthews, Lois Kimball, 5-6
Matthews, Richard, 124
Mayflower Compact, 29
McCullough, David, 122
McKinley, Albert E., 75-76
McKitrick, Eric, 11
Miller, Perry, 11
moderator, 20-21, 23
Monkkonen, Eric H., 10
Montgomerie Charter of 1731, 52
Munroe, John A., 78

natural rights, ix, 2, 7, 15, 119, 126, 128, 134-136, 139-140, 143, 148
Nevins, Allan, 81

New Amsterdam, 52, 55
New England town: drinking, 143; taverns, 93-95, 97, 102-105; virtues, 88, 92-93, 99, 101, 105, 118-119
New England village, 89-90, 92
New Hampshire: president, 29; Protestant faith, 30
New Jersey: chambers, 57; *Declaration of the True Intent and Meaning*, 58; *Fundamental Constitutions of 1683*, 58
Newport, RI, 3, 35, 36, 44, 48, 55
New Urbanist, 89
New York: apprenticeship, 55; board of trustees, 54; *burgomasters*, 52; Court of Assizes, 56; Dongan's Charter, 52; Duke's Laws, 52; poverty relief, 54; *schepens*, 52; *schout*, 52
New York City, NY, 47, 52, 55-56, 59, 77
Norby, Chris, 151
Normans, 5
North Carolina, 68
Northwest Territory, 91
Notes on the State of Virginia, 88

O'Neill, Thomas Tip, 150
Oglethorpe, James, 71-72
Osgood, Herbert, 10, 31, 39, 41-43, 45, 70, 72, 75-81
ostracism, 8
outlivers, 33

parish system, 50
Patriot Act, 144-145
Peden, William, 120
Penn, William, 60-61
Pennsylvania: constable, 60: justice of the peace, 59-60; similarity to Delaware, 61
Pequot War, 16
Percival, John, 71-72
Pestana, Carla Gardina, 11
Philadelphia, PA, 3, 48, 59, 75, 87, 94, 120, 145
phlip, 94, 105
Plymouth, 29

Poletown Neighborhood Council v. Detroit, 136
Poletown, MI, 135-136
Polishook, Irwin H., 76
poll tax, 38, 63, 65, 69, 70
polycentrism, 49
Pomfret, John E., 77
poundkeeper, 53
Powell, William S., 80
Princeton, 137
private organizations, 48
private property, 2-3, 138
Progressives, ix, xi, 139, 143, 148
property requirements, 30
property rights, x, 3, 126, 136, 139, 148
property tax, 38, 68-69, 87
proprietors, 17-18, 32, 57-59, 61, 68, 71-72, 77
Providence Plantations, 34
public whippings, 8
Puritans, 7-9, 19, 118
Putnam, Robert D., 151

Quaker troubles, 19
Quakers, 58
Queen Anne, 57-58

rebellions, 51
Reeves, Mavis Mann, 11, 117, 124
Regulator's Revolt, 51
religious liberty, 2, 15, 48, 126
representatives, 16, 29, 54, 87, 106-110, 134
republic, 9, 110-114, 116-119, 125-127, 133, 141, 143, 148
republican, 125-126
Reynolds v. Sims, 134, 150
Rhode Island: almshouses, 36; church and state separation, 35; eminent domain, 32, 35; poor relief, 36; punishment, 36; voter turnout, 34; workhouses, 36
Riordon, William L., 151
Rubin, Louis, 75, 79
rule by the majority, 7
rum, 72, 94, 102, 110
Russia, 7

Savannah, GA, 72, 146
Saxon government, 5, 6, 128-129
Seiler, William H., 80
Selby, John E., 79
selectmen, 21-22, 25-27, 33, 35, 38, 96, 106-107
September 11, 127, 141-142
Seybolt, Robert Francis, 10, 77
sheriffs, 79, 84-88
Sirmans, Eugene H., 80
Sly, John, 20, 39, 40-41
Smith, David A., 81
Smith, Page P., 10-11
social cohesion, 7
Social Darwinism, 6
Sons of Liberty, 56
South Carolina: duties, 69-70; parish, 69-70; settlements, 70; taxes, 69-70
Stamp Act, 96-98, 102, 105, 133
state of nature, 127, 129-131, 140
Stuart, James, 57
Stuyvesant, Director, 55
Surrender from the Proprietors of East and West New Jersey, 59
Syrett, David, 40, 122

Tate, Thad W., 79
tax collection, 24, 49, 54, 73, 81, 85
tax list, 24, 63
Taylor, Robert J., 39, 44
Ten Commandments, 148
terrorism, 130, 141-142
Thoreau, Henry, 90
tithingman, 22-23, 38
Tocqueville, Alexis de, 1-2, 10, 98-100, 122, 132, 143, 149, 174
Town Act of 1636, 14
town democracy, 20, 95-96, 100
town meeting: participation, 20, 31, 51, 96, 125, 132, 139; poor attendance, 20, 34, 98
town membership, 99-100
town officers, 22-23, 29, 32
Townshend Acts of 1767, 56
township, 1-2, 48, 53-54, 59-60, 62, 73, 76, 98-99, 112, 115, 139, 148

Turner, Frederick Jackson, 6, 10-11
Tyler, John, 111
tyranny of the majority, x, 2
Varga, Nicholas, 52, 75-77
Virginia: county justices, 65, 67; courts, 65-67; House of Delegates, 85; sheriff, 66-67
voting, methods of, 21

Wall Street Journal, 136
Wallace, Mike, 56, 75-77
Walpole, Sir Robert, 71
War on Terror, 127
wards, 52, 111-118, 125
Warner, Sam Bass, Jr., 39, 75
Washington, George, 84-85, 120
Waterhouse, Richard, 80
Weir, Robert M., 81
welfare, 26
West, Thomas G., 11
Wheeler, Robert, 79-80
Williams, Roger, 34
Willingham, William F., 43
Wilson, James, 6, 10, 78, 85, 120, 128-129, 150-151
Winter, William O., 40, 75, 122
Wood, Joseph, 89-90, 121
Wright, Louis B., 81
Wythe, George, 86

Yarbrough, Jean, 116, 123

zoning, 2, 136-137, 140
Zuckerman, Michael, 11, 22, 40-41
Zuckert, Michael P., 11, 117, 124

❋ ❋ ❋